THE TROUBLE WITH FATE

THE FORBIDDEN LOVE SERIES

KAT T. MASEN

Kat T. Masen

The Trouble With Fate

A Best Friends Brother Romance
The Forbidden Love Series Book 5

ISBN: 979-8435197358

Editing by More Than Words Copyediting and Proofreading
Cover design by Outlined with Love Designs
Cover Image Copyright 2022
First Edition 2022
All Rights Reserved

This book is dedicated to Tash.
Fly high, sweet angel.

BLURB

I am nothing like my sisters.
The Edwards' daughters have a reputation for falling in love under forbidden circumstances.
Not me, though.
I'm the calm, collected one and Daddy's new favorite since I cause the least trouble.
This is all thanks to my long-time best friend, Cruz Cooper.
He's every bit the crazy person I'm not and keeps me grounded with college despite his wild ways.
We have all these plans to live off-campus, then start our careers without wasting our best years caught up in toxic relationships.
Until the night we had dinner with his parents.
And his older brother walked in...
Masen Cooper.
He looked nothing like I remembered. Tall, muscular—sexy in ways I prefer not to think about. Yet five minutes spent with him, and he is clearly still the arrogant jerk who would taunt me as a kid.
Now, he has his eyes on me once again.
But this time, he wants to play a different type of game.
One which will force me to choose between two brothers...

"But fate knew something we didn't." - Unknown

PROLOGUE

MASEN COOPER

Ten years ago

"C'mon, Ava. Dad will *kill* you."

Amelia crosses her arms inside the Edwards' den while warning her sister with an ignited stare. The emerald-colored eyes the Edwards family is known for shine brightly, almost illuminating the room like they hold power to change the energy in just one look.

Ava continues to half hang her body across the couch, passing her phone to show me a video of some guy puking after drinking beer from a boot. We both laugh, ignoring Amelia until she clears her throat, demanding attention.

"He won't find out," Ava drags, uninterested in her older sister's worry. "It's just a party, and I promise I won't come back drunk like last time. Vodka isn't my friend."

"Neither is tequila," I snicker.

Amelia continues to grind her teeth in frustration. "Last time, I had to make up some elaborate lie which almost landed me in trouble. You know I hate lying to Dad, and this time, I won't cover for you."

Jensen Alcott throws the most wicked parties. Since he's an only child and his parents are always traveling, the parties are always unsupervised. At the last one, the cops were called to his Bel Air property and arrived when I was fucking Harlow Alcott, Jensen's cousin. Even though we heard the yelling, I still managed to finish through the chaos with only seconds to pull my jeans back up and toss the condom to the corner. To add to the accomplishment, I was *that* good even Harlow came.

Ava and I frequent the same scene because we go to the same school plus are close in age. Also, our parents are good friends, so I've known Amelia and Ava pretty much all of my life.

Tonight, the girls' father, Lex, and my dad are drinking out on the patio celebrating some business deal. According to Ava, our moms are trashed too, which is why all of us kids ended up in the den, avoiding the drunken rants of our parents.

My brother, Cruz, is four years younger than me, and no surprises at all, he's watching the football game on the large television screen. His obsession with the game continues to confound me. That's coming from someone who can't care less about sports. Not unless it's two hot chicks wrestling in a mud pit. *Fuck, maybe I should text Harlow and see if she's going to be at the party tonight.*

I quickly send a text, only for Ava to catch a glimpse of the message and my choice of dirty words. A smirk plays upon her lips, but then she goes back to texting on her phone.

"Okay, so Jensen's bestie, Taylor, will pick us up in ten minutes behind the bush where the camera doesn't point."

Pressing my lips together, I hide my amusement. Ava has her security system memorized. This isn't her first sneak-out, and it won't be her last. It'll only be a matter of time before her father finds out, then we're all dead meat. But for now, who cares if we break the rules.

"Well, I'm informing you officially. I won't lie to them," Amelia tells her sternly.

A sigh escapes me. "Look, Amelia, if it makes you feel better, I'll go with her."

Amelia snorts. "Which girl's pants are you trying to get into tonight?"

I glare at Ava. Only she knew who I slept with. Ava shrugs her shoulders as if she didn't open her big fat mouth to her sister.

"Don't look at me," Ava is quick to call out. "Everyone knows you're the school jerk. Act like you can't stand them, then find yourself in a hate fuck."

Sitting beside Cruz is Amelia and Ava's younger sister, Addison. Their youngest sister, Alexa, is at some sleepover, and thank God because the little brat is annoying.

Addison Edwards rarely says a word. She's an observer with her head constantly buried in a book. Only tonight, I noticed she's changed and no longer a scrawny middle-school kid. She looks similar to Ava, the same shade of brown hair, unlike Millie, who has lighter hair like her mother.

Her face has thinned out, but her body makes her look older than someone in junior high. I'd overheard Ava earlier tonight teasing Addison about just how much attention she'll get in senior year with her chest. I swear Ava is the sister you pray never to have.

Cruz rolls his eyes at the comment, barely paying attention since the score is a tiebreaker. He's sitting at the edge of his seat in anticipation, his hand curled into a fist and pressed up against his mouth.

"See, Masen will come with me. I can't get into any trouble. Besides, Addy can cover. Right, Addy?" Ava moves toward Addison, placing her arms around her affectionately. "What are sisters for?"

"Your harmful influence is referred to as manipulation," Addison simply says without removing her eyes from the pages in the book.

Ava pulls back. "Okay, Dr. Edwards, we get it. You want to become a psychologist and fix everyone's problems. My problem right now can easily be avoided if you simply tell Mom and Dad I have period cramps and fell asleep early."

I cringe at the *period cramps*. Why do girls have to mention shit like that?

"Ava, she's right. Stop pressuring her for your own selfish reasons," Amelia scolds her.

My eyes fixate on Addison, and for a brief moment, her gaze flicks up at me, only for her to panic and drop her eyes back between the book. If I didn't know better, I'd say her cheeks are turning a crimson red.

She's always been an easy target, and even though she spends a lot of time with Cruz, it doesn't mean it's not fun to torment her when she's around. It's not my fault I'm bored, and the only entertainment is making her squirm.

"Why don't you join us, Addison?" I continue to watch her, intending to make her uncomfortable, so she cracks and covers for us. "Surely, you must be into boys now?"

Ava laughs at the same time Cruz takes his eyes off the screen. "Hey, Jerk. Leave her alone."

No surprise, my baby brother is all protective over his best friend. If I want to, I can make this kid's life hell. The kid is a damn pussy.

Actually, I want to.

"Worried some older guy is going to take your girl from you?"

Cruz's nostrils flare, his focus no longer on the precious game. He flexes his arm muscles, preparing himself like he can take me on. I may not play sports religiously like him, but I enjoy spending time with my dad at the gym every morning. Besides, the girls love my body. At least that's what they like to tell me when underneath me naked.

Slowly, he turns his head, so our eyes meet. He plants his feet on the floor, standing up, then takes a step toward me as I stand up as well. I'm one of the tallest boys in our year, so why he thinks he can fight me is beyond me right now.

His stare is cold and flinty, my words triggering him like always.

"You may be my brother by blood..." he begins with an arctic tone, "... but believe me when I say I'll always protect my best friend over you."

"C'mon, baby bro," I tease with a smirk. "Will you relax? We're just having fun. Stop acting like I'm going to steal your girlfriend from you."

The second the words leave my mouth, Cruz's arm swings at me to punch my face, but I grab his wrist just in time.

"What's your problem?" I ask him in annoyance.

Cruz tries to shake his arm out of my grip with no luck. "My problem is always you."

"C'mon, guys," Amelia begs softly. "Let it go."

"Yeah, Addy can defend herself," Ava butts in. "And, Cruz, for the record, wait until you're in college and trying to protect her. You'll be up against every guy with how beautiful she is."

Addison continues to sit quietly, but then she closes her book, directing her eyes onto my moron of a brother.

"Cruz, I can defend myself, but thank you for always having my back," she says with sudden confidence. Then, her gaze shifts to me. "As for your comment of stealing me from Cruz, I'd rather bathe in a pile of dog shit than ever be your girlfriend. At least with dog shit I won't catch a sexually transmitted disease from all the whores you sleep with."

Ava bursts out laughing, placing her hand on my shoulder for comfort.

Amelia tries to hide her smile. As for Cruz, of course, he's gloating.

I continue to stand here, furrowing my brows over her distaste toward me. Not like I fucking care. She's fourteen, and I don't care whatsoever for girls this young. I stick to my own age, seventeen and sometimes above if I lie and say I'm older.

I have the perfect comeback inside my head but decide against it. I'm not going to waste my breath when Taylor will be outside with his Jeep in a few minutes.

"Let's go, Ava. I've had enough playtime with the kids."

Ava punches my arm, causing me to scowl.

As for Addison, she goes back to her book but not before glancing at me one more time. She may have won for now, but I swear, one day, I'll get her back for that comment.

The moment she least expects it...

ONE

ADDISON

Present

The crowd is cheering loudly in the stands.

We're packed in like sardines, bumping shoulders at the edge of our seats as the scoreboard continues its countdown.

There's nervous energy amongst us, several fans closing their eyes and mumbling some sort of prayer to the polar opposite, and profanities being yelled against the already loud noises coming from the stadium speakers.

Our team is killing it. Although I don't consider myself a huge sports fan, I came for the buzz. From the loud music blasted each time a team scored to the exhilaration and adrenaline that pumped through the crowd, the chants unite strangers as we sway, arms around our neighbors with a sense of pride.

Inside my pocket, my phone buzzes again. Not wanting to miss anything important, I quickly pull it out to see my sisters and cousins' group chat out of control once again. It's not unusual for me to mute our conversations, especially when I'm trying to study or do anything productive.

> **AVA**
> I want updates, Addy. Any hot guys at the game?

> **MILLIE**
> You're married.

> **JESSA**
> Ohhh... yeah. Updates please.

> **LUNA**
> YOU ALL HAVE MEN

> **AVA**
> I'm looking for potential life partners for Addy.

> **JESSA**
> Luna... you need to get laid.

> **LUNA**
> I'm satisfied, ladies. I don't need a man.

> **AVA**
> Or pussy?

> **MILLIE**
> Oh God... Ashton just saw that, and I had to tell him you were looking at adopting a cat.

> **AVA**
> Meow... hahahaha

A laugh escapes me, but instead of defending Luna, I quickly type back to save myself from Ava's obsession with my dating life. I almost preferred it when she was single and too busy to focus on anyone else.

ME

I'm busy supporting my best friend. And for the record, I can find my own man and preferably one who isn't drenched in sweat giving his friend a wedgie.

The messages in the chat continue to appear, none of them relenting, so I place my phone back in my pocket and ignore the girls to focus back on the field.

My eyes wander to where Cruz is standing with a serious expression. Even with the helmet on, his body language appears frustrated with the way his hands rest on his hips while his coach yells from the sideline.

Sixty seconds are left on the clock, each number drawing down with the pressure mounting. The beat of my heart is drumming so loud, ready to burst through an oversized jersey I'm wearing. Any second now, it will splat onto the floor in front of me as I bounce on my toes, unable to control my movements from the build-up of anticipation.

Even though they were in the lead, the final buzzer will dictate the official winner.

C'mon, guys. You can do this.

I'm biting my nails, a habit I broke in middle school only to pick up again at moments such as this. The pressure is killing me, so I shift my gaze away from the scoreboard and back onto Cruz.

He's in his element—game face on and ready to kill. He's cute when he's in game mode but don't get me wrong, there's no harboring of romantic feelings toward him.

Cruz is my best friend, that's all.

We're close, just not in the way everyone assumes, and when I say everyone, I'm referring to my overbearing family. Growing up in a family with sisters only, Cruz is the brother I've never had.

If only I had a dollar for every time I've had to clarify that, I'd probably be as rich as my *father*. The great Lex Edwards as he's referred to. I don't know why people jump to conclusions when no one really questioned Andy and Jessa when they were close.

Cruz is a good family friend and has been for as long as I can remember. His parents, Haden and Presley, are super tight with my parents. They even have business ventures together.

People—and I mean my sisters—need to mind their own damn business. Of course, when they found out Cruz and I were going to UCLA, it stirred the so-called thoughts inside their close-minded brains. I want to major in psychology with the flexibility to visit home when I feel like it. As for Cruz, he got accepted into the Bruins football program.

This is his last year, making this game bittersweet like all of them as we draw closer to the end.

As I continue to observe my best friend and his body language, the pressure is getting to him. He lives and breathes the game, a typical jock, of course.

I don't do the whole jock thing, unlike every other girl on campus. Give me a guy wearing a plaid shirt, glasses, and into literature over bulky torsos and man sweat any day. I like the quiet ones, not the obnoxious drink-a-keg-and-show-off-by-burping-the-alphabet type of guy.

Cruz falls somewhere in the middle.

He's intelligent and gets good grades but is the biggest dick around his friends, including me. Girls love him, of course. He has the whole golden blond waves and blue-eyed thing happening plus one dimple indented in his left cheek which girls go stupid over.

But unlike all the other jocks, Cruz is somewhat picky with the women he hooks up with, and lately something's been off. He rarely mentions or jokes about other girls, almost as if someone or something has gotten to him.

The buzzer finally rings loudly, distracting me from my thoughts. The stand of supporters jumps in the air to cheer the team's victory win.

"YES!"

I fist pump the air, screaming at the top of my lungs until I fall into a fit of coughs from my dry throat. My arms unknowingly throw themselves over the girl beside me, hugging her tight while we continue to holler proudly.

Some guy, a big unit on my left, removes his jersey and starts smacking his chest like Tarzan. The stomping is in sync, and in the middle of the first verse, I'm suddenly surrounded by half-naked men singing their victory song.

My eyes scan the huddle for Cruz. It takes me a few moments to find him, given the crowds of people who have raced onto the field. Our gaze meets, his broad smile lighting up his entire face. Despite the distance between us, he fist-pumps me, and I do so in return. I'm crazy proud of him. This win will give him opportunities beyond college. Finally, he'll be able to follow his dream and play for the big leagues.

Abandoning my chair, I run down the steps with excitement, careful not to lose my balance. Squeezing through the gate like many others are doing, I run toward Cruz, tackling his body from behind. Bad idea, my body slams against the hard padding causing me to wince. He turns around, wearing a smile filled with pride and laces his arms around my waist to lift me in the air.

"Can you believe it, Addy? We fucking won!"

I throw my arms around his drenched neck.

"You totally killed it, kid. We're so partying up big time tonight. Pizza, movie, whatever you want to do."

Cruz drops his head with a chuckle. "How many years

have you been at college, and your idea of partying is still pizza and a movie?"

My lips purse, waiting for this lecture. I'm not exactly one to eat junk food and prefer a salad over the grease that passes off for food these days.

"Pizza is partying when you don't exactly eat it every day."

"I have a better idea, party at Jacob's parents' house," Cruz insists as I begin to cringe. "You better do shots with me this time. Plus, we have yet to celebrate the apartment we found, roomie."

"I'm going to ignore the peer pressure and agree to drink as your best friend. Therefore, my decision is to get wasted and not on your terms. And yes, our fabulous apartment needs to be celebrated."

"Which part? The massage parlor next door or the Indian restaurant downstairs?"

"We both love Indian food, so that's a tick," I say with a grin, then I cross my arms. "The massage parlor is all you."

The corners of Cruz's lips pull into a smirk. "I'm offended you think I'm that type of man."

Coach Rancic calls Cruz's name. College journalists covering the story surround him.

"Oh, man, I better get this shit over with," he complains, narrowing his eyes in annoyance. "Okay, my place at seven. Don't be late, and don't wear that skanky black dress that flashed your ass last time. I'm not spending the whole night being your bitch slave and fighting off jerks."

"Wow, calling your best friend a skank is a great way to start celebrations."

I recall the memory of having nothing to wear and allowing Ava to dress me. There was no time to change, and as someone who doesn't wear dresses often, especially tight-fitting bodycon dresses, I spent most of the night making sure my ass wasn't on display.

"Okay, you go." I turn him around, pushing him toward the coach. "Love you! And I'm proud of you!"

Cruz turns around, reaching out his hand then retracting it against his chest and resting it on his heart. Teasingly, he bites his lip, unable to tame his proud grin. "Love you too, Addy."

TWO

ADDISON

Mom's red velvet cake is watching me.

I'm sitting on the wooden stool with my elbows resting on the marble countertop, eyeing the cake as if it were my nemesis. The nerves crippled my appetite earlier on. That, and the smell of sweaty men and corndogs was the least bit appealing.

The soft white icing looks mouth-watering, teasing me with its sugary existence. Mom has this secret to making the best icing I've ever tasted. Sure, I'm biased because the woman can do anything. Yet there's not one person I have come across who has ever said no to tasting her red velvet cake.

"Just eat the damn cake," Alexa chastises while braiding her hair away from her face.

She's wearing denim cut-off shorts and platform white sneakers. The gray t-shirt she wears is a relaxed fit, with the hem length covering the frayed shorts. If Dad sees this, he'll have a coronary. Ava used to push the limits with her short attire, but Mom always got to her first before Dad ever saw her.

"I shouldn't," I answer with a head shake. "The last thing I need is a sugar high after all the excitement from today."

Alexa rolls her eyes at me. "Why do you have to overanalyze everything?"

"I'm not overanalyzing," I argue back, biting my lip as I try to resist reaching out to it. "It's been a big day, and my adrenaline is finally evening out. The last thing I need is to be filled with sugar, to which there will be zero chance of sleeping tonight."

"Didn't you say you were going to some party with Cruz?"

"Yes, but we know he'll find some girl to hook up with, which is great because I can sneak out early," I tell her with ease. "Besides, I'm watching this documentary on Wall Street which is so fascinating."

Alexa busies herself on her phone. "Uh-huh. Okay, Dad."

The moment the words escape Alexa's mouth, Dad strolls into the kitchen talking on the phone. Judging by the serious expression on his face, I'm assuming it's a business call until he softly mentions Mom's name followed by a sigh.

"I have to go," he says, eyeing us. "I have two daughters about to go head to head over the last piece of your cake."

I shake my head to whisper, "Not me."

"I'll see you soon, love you too." Dad hangs up the call and tucks the phone into the pocket of his pants. "Now, you do know it's quite a large slice which we can slice into three equal parts so all of us can taste your mother's sweet perfection."

Alexa snorts as my lips press flat to stop myself from laughing. If Ava were here, she'd vocalize just how gross that sounded. God, I miss her sometimes.

A wide grin appears on his face as he rubs his chin. He's usually freshly shaven, but today he has a slight stubble. Just like always, he's dressed in a tailored suit. As much as it pains me to say it, Dad is a very handsome man. Yet much like my sisters, we avoid how his 'looks' have gained him a fanbase of women. It's disturbing to see such vulgar posts attached to shirtless pics of Dad when he was younger.

"Okay..." he begins, then stalls, "... that didn't come out as intended."

"I have no idea what you're talking about," I respond innocently.

Alexa simply shakes her head, suppressing her laughter.

Dad lets out a heavy sigh. "Ava Edwards has truly left her mark in this household."

"Ava Edwards-Carter," I correct him. "Your little trouble-maker is all grown up now though you wouldn't think so if you read our group chats."

His brows raise at the mention of Ava's behavior. Then, he laughs softly. "So, about this cake?"

I pull a knife out of the drawer to slice the cake into three pieces just like he suggested. Alexa retrieves three spoons for us to use. When the cake is divided evenly, we all dig our spoons in and take our first bite. We eat in silence, each one of us quietly praising Mom for her efforts once again.

"Mom outdid herself," I say with a mouthful.

Alexa nods in agreement. "We say this every time."

"But this time, I mean it. And stupid me was trying to resist."

As we devour the cake rather quickly, Dad makes himself a coffee since it's late afternoon. He's an early riser just like Mom. They both wake up at the crack of dawn to start their workday.

I take up his offer for one, too, since I woke up early as well and today was chaotic with the game.

Dad slides the mug over as we sit at the counter together.

There's never a right time to bring up the topic of moving in with a guy, even if the guy is your best friend. Though, I find the courage to do so now for fear of it leaking out another way and my parents finding out from someone else.

"I know Mom isn't here, and we usually discuss these things together, but I wanted to let you know I'm moving out of my apartment.

"Oh?" Dad tilts his head to the side. "What's wrong with your apartment now?"

"They tore down the building next door, so all I can hear is construction. It's frustrating when I'm trying to study."

"Well, you know you're always welcome back home," Dad kindly offers. "And I never liked the idea of you renting. I'd prefer it if you allowed us to buy you a place."

I place my hand on his. "I know, Dad, but I got this. I need to learn how to balance work and studying. It's what builds life skills. It's important for me to be responsible for my life, and that includes paying rent."

"Why don't you tell Dad about your other plan?" Alexa goads with a smile.

My eyes dart to hers with annoyance. This time, Dad crosses his arms while waiting for me to elaborate on Alexa's comment.

"So, I'm planning on getting a roommate."

"A roommate?" he repeats cautiously. "Do I know this person?"

My hands wrap around the mug as I bring it up to my lips and blow the steam before taking a sip. "You do. It's Cruz."

"I see," he answers in a flat voice.

I watch him with curiosity. "I see as in you have a problem with me living with a male or I see because it's Cruz?"

Alexa gazes at both of us a little too eagerly, which Dad notices.

"Alexa, would you mind if your sister and I have a word in private?"

"Oh, c'mon, Dad. There are no secrets in our family," she points out. "Aside from when Millie was screwing Will or Ava getting knocked up by Austin."

"Alexa," Dad warns as the muscles in his neck stiffen. "I'm asking to have a conversation in private."

Annoyed, she crosses her arms then leaves the room, mumbling something I can't make out. Dad notices her shorts then lowers his head in disappointment. He goes to open his mouth but quickly closes it, focusing his attention back onto me.

My relationship with Dad has always been easy. My sisters and I had watched Millie and Dad butt heads often. So, when her relationship with Will came out, we all thought she had hooked up with him to get back at Dad or something. It turns out she was in love. I mean, who would've thought? Not me, yet it all made sense when I actually saw them together as a couple.

As for Ava, she's Dad's favorite though he's never said it out loud. The bottom line is she got away with everything. When she got into trouble in high school, she'd somehow sweet-talk Dad, and he barely punished her. That, and she knew how to get us girls to cover for her to lessen the punishment.

Being the youngest of all, Alexa seems to be under the radar. I know she is Ava 2.0 but is careful with keeping her social life as private as possible. She knows how to produce good grades given it's her senior year and somehow still manages to maintain her friends plus God knows what else she does.

Though with me, I've never been one to sneak out and party while living here. I studied, enjoyed reading, and loved learning from Dad. The man is brilliant, and even as his daughter, his life still fascinates me.

Yet as he sits across from me with a stern gaze, I suspect his wanting to talk in private will not work well in my favor.

"Addison, you know I have no ill feelings toward Cruz. He's a good kid..." he begins with, choosing his words carefully, then continues, "I just think his lifestyle isn't suitable for the path you're choosing to embark on."

His concern comes as no surprise, especially since Cruz is a known party boy. Being around jocks has him set in his ways. However, I consider myself my own woman. Just because he chooses to party hard doesn't mean I have to. Aside from tonight, I didn't always say yes to going out with him. In fact, my reluctance often caused fights between us. Over time, Cruz got over himself when he realized I had no problem standing my ground.

"I get it, Dad. I really do. But trust me when I say our agreement to become roommates wasn't without setting rules and boundaries. Cruz can party as hard as he likes outside, just not bring it back to the apartment. As for women, well, I've made it clear he is responsible for strangers and their actions should he choose to bring them back."

Dad nods quietly, his gaze unwavering. "And what about you? How would he feel should you have a gentleman caller?"

I burst out laughing. "Gentleman caller? We both know I'm not like that."

"You're most certainly not," Dad concurs with a proud smile. "I don't pick favorites with my daughters, but you definitely have not aged me."

The door opens as I place my hand on Dad's reassuringly. Mom enters the kitchen dressed in her work attire. The woman looks gorgeous in anything, but today, red looks fantastic on her.

Her usually vibrant face appears flat until her gaze falls upon mine for a smile to grace her lips.

"Addy." She sighs before she leans over to kiss Dad hello. He glances at her with a worried expression while something passes between them. "Please tell me you're staying for dinner?"

I quickly check the clock on the wall, calculating the hours with the conclusion that Cruz can start the night without me.

"Of course, Mom." She moves into where I sit, hugging me from behind tightly. "Is everything okay?"

"It's been a tough day," she answers with resignation. "So, having you here is exactly what I need."

My shoes push against the counter wall to swivel around to face her. As I try to read her expression, she runs her finger down my cheek with a grin.

"My little psychologist is trying to read Mommy's face." She laughs then cups my chin. "I promise you, the emotions I'm feeling right now are normal when handling a tough adoption case."

I tilt my head sympathetically. "I'm here to listen if that will help."

"Thank you, sweetheart, for the offer. To be honest, I just want to come home and see my family. It's the best stress reliever I can ask for."

"Of course." I grab her hand to squeeze it tight. "But how about I cook? You and Dad go get some wine and relax outside on the patio. It's been a while since I burned something, so chances are, we'll have something edible."

My parents both chuckle then breathe a sigh of relief.

"I'll go to the cellar and grab us the bottle of red Haden and Presley brought back from Australia," Dad informs Mom.

"Sounds like a plan. I'm going to shower and get changed," Mom says, then glances my way. "You sure you don't need help?"

"I got this, Mom."

———

The sun begins to set on the horizon as we eat out on the patio admiring the view.

My parents purchased this house when Millie was born, and all of us girls grew up in the house. The truth is, I can't imagine calling any other place home.

When I moved out and into a dorm room, the small space made me extremely claustrophobic. It's why I spent most of my time in class or the library, using the dorm room to only sleep. On weekends, I'd come back home because it was more comfortable.

Then, when I moved into my apartment, it was much nicer and bigger but still didn't feel right.

However, sitting here, gazing at the canyon and breathing in the serenity, I know that nothing will ever compare.

Alexa had some birthday dinner to go to though truthfully, she looked way too good for a birthday dinner. If I didn't know better, she was off to meet some guy. As long as she doesn't get knocked up, I don't care what she does.

"You've outdone yourself," Mom compliments, raising her wine glass.

I raise my glass as does Dad, the three glasses clinking together. It isn't often the three of us have dinner together, but it's something I enjoy immensely.

"Well, I did learn from the best."

"That, I'll second." Dad nods in agreement. "Charlotte has always been an amazing cook."

"You weren't so bad yourself when we first got married. Even better when I was pregnant with Millie and had all these weird cravings." Mom laughs.

Dad grins at the memory. "Sandwiches, though the fillings were questionable."

"Oh?" I turn to gaze at them in amusement.

"I wanted Chinese takeout inside sandwiches. But your father, being worried about all the ingredients, tried to make healthier versions."

He drops his head with a soft chuckle. "I tried, but I knew when I went to work, you convinced Eric to visit our local Chinese takeout place."

"Okay, so maybe I did..." she admits with a smirk, "... but it wasn't without a lecture on cankles."

I shake my head with a small huff. "Eric and his obsession with cankles."

"I saw him eyeing your sisters when they were pregnant. I warned him if he opened his big fat mouth, I'd tell everyone he caught crabs at the gym, which is why he couldn't come to Adriana's birthday party."

My hand moves to my chest in disgust. "He caught crabs at the gym? Is that possible?"

"When you accidentally use someone else's towel."

"Ew," I groan.

Dad rolls his eyes with boredom. "Change of subject, please. So, Addison, maybe you should mention to your mother what you told me earlier?"

Mom places her wine down, watching me with curiosity. Her ability to listen and read someone's mannerisms is from years of being a lawyer. She's a patient person, always waiting for all the facts to then make an informed decision.

"The long story short is that I'm moving. Cruz is going to be my roommate."

I observe her reaction, but unlike Dad, she isn't as concerned.

"You're an adult, and I know you're responsible," is all she says.

"Is that all you're going to say?" Dad questions her.

"Yes, because she's not Ava or Alexa," Mom reminds him with a forced smile. "Addy has proven she's focused. End of story."

"A little unfair to Amelia, don't you think?" Dad argues, though his tone isn't raised or confronting. "She was treated differently."

Mom crosses her arms in defiance. "That was your fault with your overbearing protectiveness. Half the time, I had to lie to you to allow Millie some freedom."

I raise my hand to stop the potential argument. "Listen, the both of you were entering a learning phase with your children. It's common to react with heightened emotions when dealing with your eldest child. Like anything in life, with experience comes wisdom. My point is, I'm glad to be daughter number three and Dad's potential favorite."

My parents chuckle softly, drinking their wine to ease the momentary tension.

"Don't let Ava hear you say that," Mom warns in jest. "And you know we love you. You're going to do amazing things. The fact you managed to calm down your father shows just how skilled you are already."

With a satisfied smile, I fall back into the wicker chair and gaze into the sky. The swirls of pink mixed with scattered clouds are mesmerizing, and sharing it with my two favorite people makes the night even more perfect.

"I hope this job I accepted will be everything I hope it will be," I say with ease, eager to clear the thoughts lingering in my mind. "Dr. Jenner is one of the best treating psychologists in Southern California. I know I'll be pushing around a lot of paperwork, but if I want to open my own practice one day, it's best I learn from the ground up, right?"

Dad gazes at me proudly. "Understanding how the foundation holds it all together is a lesson well learned in business."

"And listen, you guys, don't worry about Cruz. He's not as bad as Haden and Presley may make him out to be. Sure, he likes to party like most guys his age, but football is his life. The game will always be his number one priority, and no one will ever change that."

"Until he falls in love one day..." Mom trails off.

An obnoxious laugh escapes me. "C'mon, Mom. He's married to the game. Nothing will break his focus. Plus, if it did, I'll be the first person to whip him back into line."

"I'd hope..." Mom pauses with a knowing smirk, "... he'll do the same for you."

I tilt my head while my parents watch with amusement. "If I ever fall in love one day, I'll think with my head and not the heart. That way, no one needs to make sacrifices which can potentially destroy a relationship in the end."

"Sometimes, Addison, your heart will not listen," Dad says with conviction.

With my shoulders straight, I pour my parents the last of the wine. I'm not a wine drinker, but of the small amount I drank, there was a certain smoothness to it.

"Dad, I promise you. Nothing will get in the way of me achieving my goals."

His emerald eyes pierce into me as if he knows some secret I don't. "You mean, no one will get in the way."

"Yes," I agree. "I bet my entire life on it."

"That's some bet, Addison," he concludes, glancing over at Mom. "I'm rarely wrong, but I hope this time I'm proven to be exactly that."

An audible breath escapes me. "Billionaire entrepreneur Lex Edwards is challenging me to prove him wrong? I mean, sure, it's not like I'm busy trying to make a life for myself."

Dad lowers his head with a smirk playing on his lips. "And if I'm right?"

With a steady gait, I extend my hand to welcome a handshake.

I don't want to say there's no chance. My interest in men is lacking. It's not like I'm swinging on the same side. It's more like I choose me.

And there's nothing wrong with that.

No matter what anyone says.

Not even the great Lex Edwards.

THREE

ADDISON

The music blares, making it impossible to hear anyone who stops by to say hello.

We walk around the Malibu mansion, aware there's glass everywhere, and no doubt something will break tonight. This isn't Jacob's first party at his parents' weekend house. The guy is notorious for his parties, plus his parents never care how trashed the place ends up because they'll easily throw money at cleaning and repairing any damage.

I recall when I was younger, Ava whining about how we'd never be able to host parties because Dad is so strict. Not only that, she would complain about why it was a waste since we were billionaires and money shouldn't be a problem.

Personally, I despise being labeled a billionaire. Sure, Dad worked hard, and so did Mom, but as for me, I'm *not* a billionaire. The label is pretentious and undeserving of someone who's still trying to graduate with her master's.

Millie is much like me, never bothered nor hung up on our family's wealth. Yet through her marriage to Will, she couldn't avoid being labeled again. Will is a self-made billionaire, another hard-working man who's deserving of everything he has strived for.

As for Ava, she's wealthy in her own right and isn't shy in vocalizing how she's worth every cent. Although, she wouldn't have gotten there as quickly without Dad's help. Something Millie points out every time they argue, leaving me caught in the middle.

"Jacob doesn't disappoint," Cruz mentions while handing me a drink. The stench is so strong my guess is the ratio of liquor is double what it should be.

The trick with parties is to nurse the drink for as long as possible without getting messy drunk. I've learned over the years to control my intake and not rush myself like everyone around me. Therefore, I'm able to control the effects of the alcohol and not do anything stupid, which I'll surely regret.

"So, we didn't get a chance to talk in the car since your dad called you."

"The man is relentless," Cruz complains while tipping back the drink and finishing it in one go. "It was a forty-five-minute lecture about how I can easily fuck up my life."

I pat his shoulder, knowing his dad's opinion is very important to him. Judging by the responses from Cruz, his dad wasn't easy on him tonight.

"He does it because he wants the best for you."

"I'm doing the best I can," Cruz strains, the creases in his forehead appearing from stress. "Okay, so there were a few mistakes today, but we won."

We walk toward the large balcony overlooking the ocean. It's much quieter here, and the ocean breeze is refreshing on this warm night. It doesn't take long for the familiar smell of weed to filter around us, which I suspect is coming from the crowd sitting on the balcony below us.

"I think, and I say this without being an expert in the

game, your dad is trying to get you to get to the core of why you made those mistakes."

A friend of Cruz offers him another drink which he takes without a second thought. I keep my opinion to myself for now, but if he drinks this as fast as the other, I won't hold back my feelings on the matter.

"Yeah, I know why. I was anxious," he admits in a low voice. "The fear of losing drove me to react too quickly."

"Right, so circling back to this fear..."

Cruz's lips curve upward into a smile. "Are we having a session right now, Dr. Edwards? I can lay down on the couch if that'll help you analyze my fucked-up brain."

I knock into his side. "I'm just trying to get you to see where he's coming from and not focus on the ideology of him busting your ass for no reason."

"I know, I know," he mumbles.

Our arms rest on the railing as we quietly watch the ocean's waves crash onto the shore. The sound is calming, despite the noise coming from inside the house.

"Anyway, what I was going to tell you is that I told my parents we're going to be roomies."

Cruz leans back, tilting his head with a stiff glance. "And I'm still alive?"

I chuckle softly. "My dad isn't that bad."

"Um, yes, he is." He nods with wide eyes. "And?"

"And nothing. We're adults, though your behavior can be questionable at times."

He digs his finger into my ribs, something he often does to annoy me because he knows I'm ticklish.

"Seriously, Addy. What did he say?"

"He trusts me, knows we're best friends, and that's it. If I was moving in with a love interest, I'm sure the reaction would've been different," I tell him honestly. "But you know I'm not like that."

Cruz shifts his gaze back onto the ocean with a smirk on his face. "Of course, Addison Edwards never falls in love."

"I'm not a robot," I inform him with slight annoyance. "What's wrong with me being single anyway?"

"You're not getting laid?"

"Yeah, well..."

"Though the offer still stands," he reminds me with a playful grin.

"Friends with benefits is the worst invention ever. Everybody knows it backfires because of jealousy or someone catches feelings while the other person is completely oblivious."

Cruz rolls his eyes at me. About a year ago, he went through a friends-with-benefits stage, which ended up exactly how I just said. He was oblivious, and the girl fell in love with him to then stalk him like a crazed maniac. He can roll his eyes all he wants, but the truth is he knows I'm right.

"Look, do me a favor and just stay single. It makes my life easier."

"Selfish much?"

"You just said what's wrong with being single? Nothing, Addy. So, you're not getting laid, big deal. That's why you've got five fingers, right?"

"Ten, actually," I correct him.

He glances sideways with a smirk. "Wow, aren't you talented? You must get off really quick."

A groan escapes me. "I'm going inside, you know, to mingle with people."

Cruz doesn't say another word, staying still while I walk inside and find a group of girls I attend classes with. The conversation begins with everyone complaining about our last paper to who's screwing who at this party.

"So, what's the deal with you and Cruz anyway?" Cherie, a ginger-haired girl, asks.

"Uh, nothing," I tell her and the other girls. "We're best friends, that's it."

"Then you don't care if I make a move?"

"Be my guest. He's not seeing anyone if that helps."

Cherie giggles, slapping my arm playfully. "Like I'd care if he was."

I press my lips flat, asking myself why I bother to interact with girls like her. At the same time, she lowers her already plunging neckline to expose the curves of her breasts. Between the top she's wearing and the short skirt sitting mid-thigh, she has definitely caught the attention of many of the men in the room.

After my wardrobe incident last time, I opted for jeans tonight with a cropped white blouse. My feet are still aching from all the standing and jumping today, so I chose to wear my wedges over a pair of heels.

"Addison, you came." Jacob extends his arms, prompting a hug.

Awkwardly, I return the gesture and allow him to wrap his arms around me. His aftershave catches my attention, the smell so masculine it stirs something within me.

Don't even think about it.

Jacob is a handsome guy. A bit preppy, but he dresses well and knows how to style himself. His ash-blond hair is combed to the side, not a single strand out of place.

"You here with Cooper?"

I nod. "Yes, he's around somewhere."

Jacob scans the room until his gaze focuses back on me. He grabs my hand and begins walking, leaving me no choice but to follow him.

We find ourselves outside again, where it's quieter and fewer people are around.

"You wanna go for a walk on the beach?" he asks, looking behind me.

"I probably shouldn't. You know because I came here with Cruz."

Jacob scratches his cheek, flinching his head back slightly. "I thought you and Cruz weren't sleeping together?"

I'm taken aback by his forwardness. "We're not."

"Then why don't you want to go for a walk?" he asks rudely.

Just as I'm about to open my mouth to answer his question as politely as I can without telling him to stick his goddamn walk up to his preppy ass, there's a rustle behind us.

"Is everything okay?" Cruz questions with a stern tone.

I take a deep breath, gazing at Cruz's sullen expression while he waits for a response. Quickly, I clear my throat to give him a proper answer without heightening the situation. There's a lot of testosterone around me, warning me to manage this as calmly as possible.

"Jacob wanted to go for a walk. I kindly declined."

On my right, Jacob huffs. His childish reaction isn't helping me diffuse this situation.

"Are you forcing her to go?" Cruz demands, moving closer to Jacob with a fierce glare. "You know the rules."

I tilt my head. "Rules?"

Jacob laughs. "Don't you know the rules? Cooper here has threatened every guy on campus. No one is supposed to touch you."

A growling noise sounds on my left. Cruz's nostrils flare as his hands clench into fists. He bows his head, trying to control himself. Despite my own anger and frustration, I need to diffuse this before Cruz punches Jacobs's face, potentially costing him his football career.

"Let's go." I grab Cruz's hand and drag him through the house until we're out the front. The second we're alone, I let go in annoyance. "What the hell did he mean when he said you've threatened everyone on campus?"

"He's talking trash," he yells back.

Cruz's raised tone is enough to know he drank more the second I walked away.

"How much have you drunk?"

"What are you, my mom?"

I let out a low whistle then take a deep breath to calm my anger. Outside, it's dark aside from the moon illuminating the sky. It's still early, though, only just past nine.

"Look, it's been a big day for you, and I'm tired. Nothing good will come from us arguing," I tell him softly. "You can stay, but I think I'm going to go home."

"Addy," he whispers. "I'm sorry, I was out of line."

"Yes, you were."

My hands fumble inside my purse for my keys. "Will you catch a ride home?"

"Don't worry. I'll be fine."

I nod quietly. Then turn around before he calls my name again.

"About what Jacob said," he begins with then stalls. "It's half true. I just don't want guys thinking you're that type of college girl."

My eyes fall to the ground. I'm not that type of girl, but if I was, the choice wouldn't even be mine. Between my father and Cruz, no man will want to go near me anyway.

"Goodnight, Cruz. Text me when you get home safely."

The car is parked just down the driveway. I walk in silence, thinking about tonight. The small window in which my attraction to Jacob came to the surface was so easily replaced by my respect toward my best friend. The more I think of it, the more I realize my lack of dating or interest in men has a lot to do with not hurting Cruz's feelings.

We've gotten into fights over guys before. One fight made me so angry I actually ended up sleeping with the guy. Cruz didn't speak to me for a whole week. It was then I realized no man was worth losing my best friend over.

Our friendship means everything to me.

As I sit in the car, the last place I want to go to is my lonely apartment. So, I take a detour and drive up the windy road toward Hidden Hills.

Pressing my sister's name on the screen, I hear the phone ring through Bluetooth.

"Hey, Addy."

"You awake?"

"I've got three kids, and I just had a baby. Always assume I'm awake," Millie retorts.

"Okay, see you in ten."

It's just after ten when I get to her place. Millie is in the kitchen with Will, sitting across from each other at the table. My eyes suddenly fall upon their plates, the red velvet cake looking awfully familiar.

"Is that where the rest of Mom's cake went?"

Millie licks her lips, and, of course, Will is gawking at her like a crazed sex maniac. Honestly, these two are trying at the best of times. How much sex can you really be having with three kids around? *Don't ask the question.*

"Yep, I snuck in early before Dad and Alexa got to it."

I plonk myself down next to Will and steal his fork out of his hand to take a bite. I'm reminded once again just how good it tastes.

"Do you think I'm heartless?"

Millie pulls back with a mouthful of cake. "I need context."

"Why are women obsessed with meeting the right guy and falling in love?"

Will grabs the fork back off me while I wait for Millie to give me her opinion on the matter. If I'd had this convo with Ava, she'd try to set me up with a string of men to attempt to change me.

"I think from a young age we're raised to believe in prince charming and the fairy tale. And during the years where we transition from girl to woman, there are so many mixed emotions. We seek validation from others, yet unsure of our own strengths. There's the whole peer pressure..."

"You mean Ava?"

Millie purses her lips, keeping her opinion on our sister at bay. "When the time is right, the time is right. Everyone is different. I mean, look at us."

I turn to observe Will, knowing he's uncomfortable should the whole 'Millie and Austin' thing get dragged up again.

"So," I say slowly, watching his reaction. "Are you saying your timing is the way you wanted it?"

"Yes," Millie answers at the same time Will says no.

Will is quick to clear his throat. "If I had my way without a certain father-in-law on my back, there would've been no break."

"And if there were no break, there would be no Ashton in our lives," Millie adds.

Will straightens his shoulders. "You have a point."

"Okay, back to me," I remind them.

"How very Ava of you," Will snickers. "Don't listen to anyone else. You do what you want to do. Don't pressure yourself to conform."

I let out a sigh, knowing Will is right. Society convinces us there's no happiness without romantic love from another person. I'm happy the way things are, so why the hell am I fixating on something because of other people's opinions. After tonight, there's even more confusion. Am I not romantically inclined because no one expresses their interest in me which has a lot to do with Cruz's threats? Or am I genuinely not programmed like every other woman I know?

"Will is right. If you fall in love, you fall in love. If you don't, you're still a worthy human being. Love doesn't have to define you. You define you."

The moment Millie finishes her sentence, one of the two baby monitors makes a sound. It's Archer talking, something about a shark and a dinosaur eating everyone. The talking stops, followed by small cries.

"Great, he's talking in his sleep again. This kid's imagination is next level." Will slides off the stool. "I'll go check on him."

Millie gazes at him lovingly, and something passes between them. I've watched them for years and know they spoke this unfounded language of love much like Mom and Dad. I think it's beautiful, but not something I can ever imagine myself feeling over someone.

"Okay, Addy. What's the real problem here?"

I shrug my shoulders. "There's no problem. It's just that every time I mention anything, everyone is quick to be all like, 'one day it will be you falling in love.' But what if I don't want that, huh? The whole heartbreak and can't get out of bed. I didn't study this hard to give up everything for a man."

"It doesn't have to be that way. Say you do fall in love, it doesn't necessarily mean it'll lead to heartbreak."

"Oh really? Tell me one couple you know who have avoided it."

Millie bites her lip while raising her eyes to stare at the ceiling as she thinks hard. The longer time passes, the more confident I am she can't name a single couple.

"Jonathan and Ellie."

"Who?"

"Friends of mine from high school. They've stayed

together since senior year. In fact, they're expecting twin girls this fall."

"It doesn't count if I don't know them," I mumble.

Millie releases a weighted sigh. "Look, Addy. You're not like Ava and me. You've always stood on your own, and there's nothing wrong with that. Just like Will said, ignore everyone. You don't need to conform, and both Mom and Dad are so proud of you. You're going to do great things, so don't sweat the stuff that isn't worth sweating because it's not on the radar."

I run my fingers through my hair then take a deep breath.

"You're right. I can control my destiny. Nothing can stop me."

Millie lowers her eyes then lifts them to gaze at me. "Maybe, but some things you can't stop."

"Like what?"

"Fate," Millie simply replies. "No one can control their own fate or the fate of others. Fate will always find a way."

FOUR

ADDISON

"You have way too much stuff."

Cruz's boxes are scattered all over our unfurnished apartment. For someone who lived in a dorm room, he sure has a lot of things. My hands reach into a box labeled *stuff*. I pull out a PlayStation remote, pair of socks, and three empty bottles of deodorant.

"This ain't all of it," he retorts.

"You mean there's more?"

He keeps quiet while tearing the tape off another box also labeled stuff. Whatever is inside, he doesn't seem interested.

"So, we're cool, right?"

"Elaborate," I say flatly.

"With the other night. I mean, I texted you, and you never responded."

Inside the next box are all of Cruz's shoes. Sneakers and more sneakers—Nike, Adidas, and Jordans. The box itself is half empty, which leads me to believe his packing skills are less than par.

"Yes, we're cool," I tell him, leaving out the part of going to Millie's to gain a female perspective on life. "I was annoyed, but you know me, give me space, and I'll come around."

The conversation ends there as we unpack in silence.

The apartment I was staying in was completely furnished. So, for now, all we have are mattresses. The actual bed frames we ordered were supposed to be delivered this morning, along with a new sofa and refrigerator. However, something happened with the truck breaking down, so our first night will be without those necessities.

Cruz brought his jumbo-sized flatscreen television, which benefits him since I never watch television anymore. When I do watch documentaries, it's usually on my phone or laptop.

And no surprises, Dad offered to find us a furnished place again and even tried to pay for it. The one thing both Cruz and I have in common is we're stubborn and want to do things for ourselves.

Cruz's phone goes off beside me as he walks to the kitchen, only to realize we have no food either. His hangry face warns of grumpy times ahead, but thankfully we have an Indian restaurant downstairs and a few decent restaurants within walking distance.

"Who texted me?" he yells from the kitchen.

I glance at his screen. "Your mom."

"And?"

I swipe the screen and enter his password, which I knew because it was his so-called lucky number. "She's inviting you for dinner tonight."

Cruz walks back in with a bottle of water then throws another to me.

"I can use a home-cooked meal, but you're coming."

I glance around the room. "But I need to unpack."

"Do it tomorrow."

"I need a shower," I complain, then lift my armpit to see if

I smell of sweat from carrying boxes up three flights of stairs. "Then get changed."

"So, do it," he drags.

"My toiletries and clothes are still packed."

Cruz releases a huff. "Okay, how about we make our beds so if we come home late, at least we can crash. I've got a meeting with Coach tomorrow, so I want to get my training session completed early."

"Sounds like a plan. I should be able to unpack a few boxes in the meantime," I say but then scowl at him. "But for the love of God, can you please move all the shoes you dumped on the floor? One of us will trip on your giant clown-size shoes, and chances are, it's going to be me."

With a slight grimace, he walks over to a pile of boxes. "Yes, mother."

A smile graces my lips as soon as I walk inside the house.

I'd visited the Coopers' home several times when we were growing up. So many great memories were made, much like my own home. Something about this house felt like home too.

Perhaps, it has something to do with Haden and Presley's love for reading. They own an expansive publishing house, so they live and breathe literature. Naturally, their home library is what I call a piece of heaven—so many talented works hidden inside the leather-bound covers. When you step into the library, there's even a particular scent that calms your soul.

"Addy," Presley calls softly from the stove as she stirs a stew that smells absolutely divine. "It's been a while."

I move toward her, leaning in to kiss her cheek then forward to inhale the aroma. My stomach makes a slight growl but thankfully isn't heard over the sound of the simmering food.

Presley is a gorgeous woman with long curly tendrils that remind me of Jessa's. I've always enjoyed spending time with her, eager to learn about what's happening with work and the authors who write for them. The publishing industry fascinates me, and I'll never get tired of listening to her talk about books.

My hands reach out for the stool, pulling it out so I can sit and talk with her. Cruz abandoned me for his gaming room, and his dad, Haden, isn't anywhere to be seen.

Presley joins me, pouring herself a white wine and one for me.

"I want to know everything that's happening with you before the boys walk in."

"Lucky, nothing is happening, so this will be quick." I grab the tomatoes in front of me and start slicing as Presley tosses the salad. "I'm working part-time while still finishing my degree. Not sure how I'll juggle it, but if Millie could do it with a husband and kid, I can do it being single."

"Fair point to make. Hopefully, my son doesn't drive you crazy and allows you time to study. By the way, is he still going out with that Fallon girl?"

"You mean Elle?" I shrug my shoulders. "I don't think so. She got all clingy, and you know him, the moment a girl clings to him, he runs a mile."

"Like father like son," Presley snickers.

"Speaking of Haden, how are things? Mom mentioned some new merger, and the both of you are working nonstop."

Presley grows unusually quiet while pouring the dressing onto the salad, but then her shoulders relax, and she releases a long-winded sigh.

"We're just as bad as each other, something we learned very early on in our marriage. So even though we're still growing as a company, I'm glad to take some time to sit back and have a break when called for. In fact, Haden and I will be traveling to the Bahamas in a few weeks for a mini vacation."

"Excuse me?" I blurt out with a serious expression. "Haden and Presley Cooper are taking a vacation? In what alternate universe have I found myself in?"

She grabs a piece of cucumber and tosses it to me with a grin.

"When your kids are grown, it's nice to unwind with your husband. Besides, Masen handles our bigger clients now."

"Apple doesn't fall far from Daddy's tree," I mutter.

"It certainly does not."

Our laughter slows down when Haden walks in with his usual smirk. Of all the men my dad is friends with, Haden is much younger and is best friends with my Uncle Noah.

Yet over the years, I'd heard Mom and Presley gossip about Haden in his younger years. The wild stallion who could never be tamed, also known as the office jerk. At least, that's what Presley often called him. They butted heads quite a lot, but apparently, it was because Haden was some sex maniac.

Oh God, why am I even reliving this conversation? The man is standing right across from me.

"If it isn't Dr. Edwards," he voices before kissing Presley on the cheek. "How much do I owe you for keeping my son grounded?"

Haden never appears to age. He's a few years younger than Presley, but neither one of them look their age. His dark hair doesn't have a single gray hair, and you can't find any wrinkles on his face. Behind his reading glasses, his eyes shine bright and are the same shape as Cruz's.

But if anything, Haden and Masen look remarkably alike from memory. Cruz is somewhat a mix of Haden and Presley.

"That's all Cruz, not me," I tell him proudly. "Your son works hard for the game."

"And I assume he's busy now, playing the PlayStation?"

"You can't take the boy out of him."

Haden excuses himself to freshen up as I continue to help Presley in the kitchen. We talk about life, my sisters, and all the new authors they've just signed up. Presley is super excited about a new author whose series hit bestseller this week.

"You must read this series. I promise you that sleep is an afterthought once you sink your teeth into this baby."

I press my lips together tightly. I'm not a reader of romances, preferring to lose myself in autobiographies.

"Is this one of your spicy recommendations? Because the last time you gave Mom something to read, Alexa caught her and Dad having sex in the jacuzzi."

Presley tries her best to hide her smile but fails miserably. "That's traumatic for Alexa."

"And me," I almost yell. "You try having your sister call you at midnight all freaked out. To make matters worse, Alexa snapped a photo which was thankfully blurry and sent it in our group chat."

"Oh God, does Charlie know this?"

"Are you kidding me? We promised never to speak of it again. My parents have no self-control."

With a sly grin, she nods in agreement. "Yeah, married couples. Annoying, aren't they?"

We finish the food preparation but not before Presley makes me search for the book on Amazon. I download it to my Kindle, at least admiring the discreet cover, so it doesn't look like I downloaded smut.

I grab four plates to take to the dining room when Presley stops me. "Oh, hun, grab another. Masen texted, and he'll be here soon."

"Oh, sure."

Just. Fucking. Great.

I'm unable to recall the last time I saw Masen. Every major family event we had, like my sisters' weddings, he's been out of the country traveling for work. If my memory serves me correctly, maybe it was at Cruz's high school graduation a few years ago.

Either way, his presence will challenge me. That's if he's anything like I remember him.

I set the table with the plates in hand as Haden and Cruz walk in arguing, of course.

"C'mon, Dad. It's all in or nothing. You said it yourself, I'm skilled, and if Coach thinks I have what it takes."

"Look, Cruz, having options doesn't hurt. It's competitive, and I just think you need to keep all your options open."

Presley looks at me, keeping quiet, not getting caught in the same argument again. The thing is, I understand Haden wanting Cruz to keep his options open. But, of course, Cruz is a loyal person, and his heart is to play here in LA and not get drafted elsewhere.

"Can we sit down and have a peaceful dinner?" Presley asks in a calm tone. "We have a guest."

"Addy is family, Mom."

I smile at him because being around the Coopers feels exactly like that in so many ways.

Haden and Cruz continue a more amicable conversation as Presley suggests we wait a few more minutes.

"Mom, I'm starving," Cruz complains.

"Honestly Cruz, you're always starving. When you were a kid—"

Presley is cut off as someone clears their throat. I turn around quickly, my gaze locking into the hazel orbs staring back at me. My chest tightens, unsure why it's happening or how it's suddenly hard to breathe normally.

"Thank, fuck," Cruz mumbles. "Can we eat now?"

Masen moves toward the seat across from me. Slowly, he removes his navy suit jacket and hangs it on the chair. Beneath the jacket, he wears a white business shirt with no tie. The top two buttons are undone, exposing a small bit of his chest. I shake my head, willing to look elsewhere.

"I didn't realize we had company," he says in a condescending tone.

"Addy isn't company," Cruz corrects him as Presley serves food onto his plate. "Addy is always welcome here."

"I never said she wasn't welcome here, brother."

"Then what's your problem?" Cruz glares at him.

Haden lets out a huff. "Seriously, let's enjoy one dinner without the two of you arguing."

Family drama isn't uncommon for me to sit through. I grew up with three sisters, all of them just as opinionated as each other. Often, Mom would also get caught in the arguments, and given that arguing is what she does for a living, she always won in the end.

Poor Dad, he usually sat there with a less-than-pleased expression while his daughters argued over hair curlers again.

I chew my food slowly, listening to Presley talk about another one of the authors they've published. Then, somewhere during a story about the author's sequel, Cruz leans over and steals a potato from my plate.

My face tilts, glancing at him with annoyance. "You know I wanted that?"

"Can't always get what you want."

I place my fork down. "Oh really? That's rich coming from the guy who almost cried because you didn't get the room with the view."

Cruz purses his lips. "There was a spider in the other room."

"Uh-huh," I mouth with a hidden smile. "According to

you, there were several spiders, a whole colony, in fact. Now, you're saying there's one? I mean, which one is it, huh? Because only one spider would mean you're a—"

"Don't say I'm a pussy."

At the end of the table, Haden wipes his mouth with a napkin, trying to disguise his smirk.

"I'd never use such a word."

Presley joins my laughter, but then, I glance across the table and into the deep stare of Masen.

His eyes are fixated on me, my face to be exact. I'm suddenly conscious there's food near my mouth. Quickly, I lick around my lips but come up with nothing. At the same time, his gaze drifts toward my mouth, and then my imagination begins to conjure up these wild thoughts. I could've sworn he bit down on his lip, but almost instantly, he lowers his head and taps on his phone's screen.

For the remainder of dinner, I avoid Masen as much as I can. Sure, he's nothing like I remember him. Instead of his usual incessant bullying, he's awfully quiet. But, perhaps, it's foolish of me to think he's the same person as when we were kids. People change, teenagers mature into responsible adults.

"I'm going to grab dessert," Presley announces after we all thank her for the amazing meal.

"Would you like some help?"

"Oh no, I need you here as referee."

The moment she leaves, Haden's phone rings, to which he lets out a groan.

"Your father will be the death of me."

A small laugh escapes me. "What has he done now?"

"You know Lex, Mr. Perfectionist," he notes with dark amusement. "Excuse me while I take this call."

Haden walks out of the room toward the kitchen, leaving just the three of us. I brace myself for the argument I'm bound to get caught in if our past is anything to go by.

"So, you still the arrogant office boy Dad likes to push around?"

And there it is...

I ignore the snarky words from Cruz, grabbing the bottle of wine and pouring myself a much-needed drink.

"Depends. Are you still the pussy jock Mom likes to baby?"

A growl escapes Cruz's lips. Why he's offended is beyond me. He started the smack talk but can't handle the comebacks.

"You know," I begin with once the wine relaxes my body, "Sibling rivalry is usually because you're fighting for your parents' attention."

Cruz leans back in his chair with confidence. "Everyone knows they love me more. I'm the miracle kid after years of trying."

Masen rests his elbows on the table, cocking his head with a sly grin. "Is that so?"

"Well, I wasn't a result of two co-workers screwing each other on a one-night stand in some club."

I clear my throat. "Actually, it was an alleyway."

The two of them shift their gazes onto me.

"What? I overhead it, I think, from Ava," I mumble, then my eyes widen on their own accord. "And something about your dad being pierced."

Oh, for the love of God, what the hell is wrong with me.

"Addy," Cruz moans, covering his face with his hands. "My dad's dick shouldn't be the topic of the Edwards girls."

"It's not topic. It was raised maybe like once."

Just as I'm about to defend myself further, Cruz's phone buzzes with a text which distracts him.

"I'll be back," he mutters as I turn to him in a panic.

"What, why?"

"Just stuff I need to sort out."

My words are trapped and too late as he exits the room as well. Slowly, my gaze shifts onto Masen since it's just the two of us.

"So, sorry about the comment, you know... about your dad."

Masen watches me with an unrelenting stare. "It appears you're fixated with such novelty."

I raise my eyebrows with a hard smile. "Such novelties don't interest me."

"How would you know unless you've tried?"

"Tried what exactly?"

He leans forward, his gaze unwavering. "Being intimate with a man who can pleasure you in the way you've never experienced before."

My eyes unwillingly explore his as I begin to grow hot and feverish. Then, with my thighs pressed together beneath the table, I keep them closed to distract myself from this unknown feeling.

"The world doesn't revolve around sex," I blurt out. "Believe it or not, there are more important and worthy matters which need attention."

Masen draws back, leaning against his chair with a smug expression. His arrogance gets on my nerves.

"If you say so, Miss Edwards."

"I mean, maybe in your world because you're such a player, that's all you think about. Some of us need more in life."

He juts his chin with a sneer. "I can guarantee, Addison, if a man satisfied you, this conversation would never have taken place."

My arms fold beneath my chest. "You're such an arrogant—"

"Jerk?" he cuts me off with a deep stare. "That's how the hate fuck always begins..."

The sound of heels clicking against the tiles distracts me as Presley walks in with dessert. The homemade cheesecake with strawberries on top looks divine. Haden is right behind Presley when I overhear him mention something about how mouth-watering they look, only for Presley to giggle and slap his arm.

Cruz's entrance is even louder. "Fuck yes, I've been missing your food, Mom."

As for me, my stomach is full of something.

Something I can't quite put my finger on.

Some may describe the feeling as fluttering, like butter-flies stuck in captivity.

And across the table, Masen continues to watch me with a profound stare. A stare so intense, I'm forced to look away to control this nonsense overcoming me. I blame our heated argument, or maybe I'm triggered by our past.

Either way, my body is betraying me.

And no chance in hell Masen Cooper is responsible for any of this.

FIVE

ADDISON

Masen left his parents' house without a goodbye.

I'd excused myself to use the bathroom, then when I returned, Cruz expressed his joy over his brother's sudden departure. Apparently, waiting five minutes to say goodbye to a guest as common courtesy is lost on the arrogant jerk.

Presley mentions something about an event he has to attend tonight, trying to defend her son. However, Haden's smirk tells a different story. But, of course, the player is busy playing his so-called field of women.

Why should I care anyway?

You don't care. Period.

With Masen gone, the tension eases, and we enjoy the time chatting about life in general. Every now and then, my mind drifts back to our conversation, to how his eyes watched me with such intent. When I find myself falling into some weird headspace, I turn to look at Cruz to bring me back to reality.

It's just after nine when we decide to leave since Cruz needs to be up at the crack of dawn for training. Presley insists we take food home, which we both welcome since we haven't gone grocery shopping yet.

Cruz wastes his breath on listing everything wrong he possibly can about his brother on the ride home. So much for trying to forget about him. Cruz is making it impossible, and their sibling rivalry only intensifies every time they're in the same space together. At least, that's what it feels like.

"The guy is so far up his ass. I swear you can't even talk to him," Cruz continues to rant, clutching at the steering wheel. "I mean, so what if he gets all the pussy. He can't hold a conversation to save his fucking life."

My gaze is fixated on the dark, windy road ahead of us. After tonight, I'm not sure what to think. Obviously, he managed to hold a conversation with me, though the topic in question was controversial. Sure, I'd never slept with a man who has a piercing, so technically, I can't have an opinion. Yet his comment on me not being satisfied was uncalled for.

I've had sex with men, four to be exact, and I can list what went wrong every time it happened. So, the conclusion is, sex is overrated.

As for Cruz's comment about all the women Masen sleeps with, it's expected, I guess, given how good-looking he is. His arrogant persona is a magnet for women though it's unhealthy and toxic if I really analyze it.

The more Cruz talks about Masen, the angrier I get. Okay, he has lots of sex. I don't care. That's why this is bothering me. It's a waste of my goddamn time and energy.

I turn to face the passenger window instead to clear my thoughts, but Cruz continues to talk without a care in the world.

"And what about his fucking comment, huh? Like he's Dad and Mom's favorite."

"That was you."

Cruz turns his head in my direction. "What, you're defending him now?"

A heavy sigh escapes me. "I'm not defending him, but you're no saint either. The moment he walked in, you started attacking and—"

"Because the guy is a jerk."

"Maybe so, but you equally contributed to the energy tonight," I tell him openly. "Now, can we stop talking about him?"

"I can't think of anything better," he mutters.

Cruz heads straight for his room when we get home, given his early morning training session. I'm not in the mood to unpack, so I take a long steaming hot shower and place my favorite PJs on. Given it's our first night here, it would've been fun to celebrate and not have him sulk in his room like a spoiled brat but say he needs to sleep for training.

Compared to my last apartment, my room is slightly smaller. There's my queen-size bed in the middle with a bedside table on each side, all of which arrived today when I was at work. My favorite mint green sheets always calm me. Something about the color is therapeutic.

The room has a small walk-in closet attached with drawers plus a small nook for my desk. All my other possessions, such as my books, are crammed in the corner until I figure out how to arrange it all.

I sit in bed and throw the comforter on top of me when my phone begins to ring. Closing my eyes for a brief moment, I take the deepest of breaths before hitting accept.

"Sister," I simply answer.

"So, any news to tell me?" Ava questions oddly.

"Um, no... I'm sitting here doing nothing."

Ava expels a loud breath. "About tonight."

"Tonight?"

"Dinner at the Coopers."

I scratch my head with confusion. "Yes, I had dinner at the Coopers."

"Oh my God, woman," Ava blurts out. "Did you tell the boys about how we know Haden is pierced?"

My head flinches back slightly, wondering how on earth she knew it came up over dinner.

"How did you know?"

"Masen."

The sound of his name stirs something odd within me again. I swallow the lump inside my throat but then remember my silence will pique Ava's curiosity.

"It was an accident."

"How does Haden's pierced dick come up by accident?"

My eyebrows squish together, trying to think of an excuse rather than admit my stupid mouth blurted it out. But, of course, I come up with nothing.

"Wait a minute," I interrupt, tilting my head in confusion. "Why would Masen tell you this? Did he just randomly call you to tell you we had dinner, and his dad's penis came up?"

"He texted me. And Addy, penis is such an unsettling word."

"Masen texted you?" I repeat as the temperature inside the room starts to rise. "So, you talk to him?"

"Well, duh. We were close for a long time."

All of a sudden, so many questions come to mind. Fact, Ava is married. I know she loves Austin, but Masen is a notorious player. *Are they having an affair?*

"Does Austin know this?"

The sound of Ava inhaling is so loud it's heard over the speaker.

"Yes, they also talk. You know, men and women can be friends without everyone thinking they're sleeping together. Look at you and Cruz."

Ava has a point, and it's presumptuous of me to think she's jeopardizing her marriage over some guy who has been in our family for years. And that's the truth, he's just someone we grew up with. He probably felt obliged to entertain tonight, or more factually, annoy me.

"You're right, sorry."

"Okay, so back to Haden's dick…"

I shake my head, though she can't see. But then I remember how much time Masen and Ava spent together as teens. Ava was never shy in admitting she enjoyed fooling around with guys, and, of course, playboy Cooper spent senior year screwing every girl he could.

"So, you've never fooled around with Masen? Not even when you guys were teens and used to sneak out to parties?"

A snort barrels through the phone. "Have you ever fooled around with Cruz? You do live together now."

"The answer is no, and just because we live together doesn't change our feelings. We'll always be the best of friends, and nothing will come between us."

"Right, so to answer your question… no, I haven't ever fooled around with Masen. He's like a brother to me."

It's my cue to abandon this conversation without raising any further suspicion. I've said too much, but my curiosity got the better of me. Ava is like an undercover FBI agent, always uncovering the truth when you least expect it.

My phone doesn't stop as the group chat starts up as soon as I hang up.

AVA

Luna, I think I found the perfect guy for you at Austin's hospital. He's an intern and totally your type.

JESSA

So old?

MILLIE

Over fifty?

LUNA

When did I ever say I liked men over fifty???
Forty is my limit.

I can't help myself typing quickly.

ME

Studies show men over fifty are more
generous in the bedroom.

LUNA

Like your dad?

AVA

WHAT IS WRONG WITH YOU!

LUNA

I'm just pointing out he's over fifty.

MILLIE

And so is your dad... dear cousin.

JESSA

Mine's forty-nine, so totally safe here.

ME

I'm abandoning this conversation. And Ava,
don't waste your time. You've got better luck
setting Luna up with patients from the
geriatric ward.

I turn all my notifications off with the hope of having
uninterrupted sleep. In the corner of my screen, my Kindle
app catches my attention. My fingers tap on the screen, then I
open the book Presley insists I read. As my eyes scan page
one, I force myself to pay attention even though romance is
my least favorite genre to read.

An hour later, the storyline gets steamy during the main
lead's encounter with her ex. The author doesn't hold back
with descriptions. She goes into great detail about how the

female lead pleasures herself because her ex reminds her of how great they were together. Amidst the dirty talk and his demanding ways, I begin to grow hot beneath the sheets.

This guy is crazy jealous, and why is this so damn hot?

A pool of wetness forms between my legs. I try to ignore my own body and its unwarranted reactions, focusing on the scene where he gets on his knees and eats her out inside an elevator.

Holy shit.

It's past midnight when I check the Kindle to see how much is left until I finish. Forty percent to go, great. Tomorrow, or should I say today, is my first day in the office. I need to be fresh and alert with the hope of making a good first impression.

Reluctantly, I place my phone down and stare at the roof in the darkness. As I beg of myself to close my eyes to fall asleep, the memories of Masen's stare continue to haunt me. The way his lips pressed together, and I wonder for a brief moment if he thought about me in any way besides Ava's sister.

My imagination takes the reins, and my body follows at its prompts. Slowly, my hand sits on my thigh, but resistance is futile. I move between my legs, grazing against my clit to expel a gasp. *Shit.* I'm brought back to reality when remembering I now have a roommate and need to keep quiet.

Yet the need to touch myself so quietly only heightens my senses. My strokes become faster, and the faster my movements, the wetter I become. The sensation spreads across my skin until my back arches, and I ride waves of the blissful orgasm.

My breathing is ragged with my eyes still shut. It takes moments to calm down, but not long after, the exhaustion weighs me down, and I find my eyes drifting to sleep.

The incessant beeping startles me.

Releasing a groan, I turn to figure out where the hell the sound is coming from to realize it's my alarm, and I'd slept past the first one.

Shit.

In a mad rush, I grab my clothes to run into the bathroom to take a shower because the delivery guys are supposed to arrive any minute now. Thankfully, I still have another hour before having to leave for my first day at work.

By the time the stupid water turns warm, I multitask, washing my hair and brushing my teeth. So much for trying to take things easy this morning. The moment I turn the faucet off, the knock on the door is loud enough to hear from the bathroom.

The towel is sitting on the rack, so I quickly grab it, dry myself, and wrap it around my body. My hair is still dripping wet, but I leave it and run out of the bathroom. As I zig zag in between the boxes, I trip on one of Cruz's shoes and fall onto the hard wooden floor.

Fuck. Fuck. Fuck.

The pain ricochets through my foot from the fall. There's a knock on the door again, forcing me to get up and hobble toward the door.

I wince in pain but quickly check the towel is covering my body. As I open the door, my eyes widen in shock.

Masen Cooper.

SIX

MASEN

Incompetent idiots.

There's no other way to describe the people sitting inside the boardroom, talking shit out of their asses like *I'm* the fucking idiot. The numbers are poor, and we're over budget. They don't realize poor performance will mean my ass is on the line too.

Lucky for them, Dad isn't sitting in on this meeting. With Lex Edwards merging more companies, Dad is busy with acquisitions which involves a fair bit of traveling.

As for Mom, her hands are also full. The editorial team is three times the size it was ten years ago. I barely see her anymore, given she balances her time between here and our other office in San Francisco.

So, I'm left with the reins and not liking what I see—weak employees who need a goddamn wake-up call.

The meeting runs one hour over the scheduled finish. By the time we end, everyone walks out in a somber mood after I give them the cold hard facts. My blood was boiling the entire time, and I'd lost my temper more than I care to admit.

It's late, almost dinner time, and the office is deserted. I send Mom a text, telling her I'm coming for dinner since I want to talk to Dad about a potential production issue. Living away from home has its perks, but damn, I miss Mom's cooking.

On the drive to my parents' place, my phone rang nonstop with urgent matters which needed attention. I find myself growing angrier by the minute, airing my frustrations through the Bluetooth while clutching the wheel and trying to control my speed. When I pull into the circular driveway, the call ends with an impromptu trip to Dallas tomorrow afternoon.

I throw my head back against the leather seat, turning the engine off to give myself a moment's peace. My shoulders are tense, and the ridge of my spine is straight. I close my eyes to ease the tension, then lean my head to the left and then the right. The slight crack is somewhat of a relief, giving me the stamina to exit the car and hopefully enjoy dinner.

As I enter the house, the kitchen is empty. There's laughter coming from the dining room, the sounds unfamiliar. I take small steps with caution, then when I turn the corner. I see the back of my brother's head.

So much for an enjoyable dinner.

Sitting beside my brother is an unfamiliar brunette. Great, a girlfriend I need to be nice to.

Mom is quick to see me, but then the brunette turns around, and emerald-green eyes meet me.

The one and only Addison Edwards.

It's been years since I last saw her—Cruz's graduation from memory. I still see Ava and Austin often, but not Addison.

The years of growing up with the Edwards girls were fun because Ava was wild and didn't care for rules. We ran the same circle and frequented the same parties, but Ava is more like an annoying sister who nags you if she doesn't get her way.

We did, however, drift apart during her time in New York, then when she got knocked up. Now that she's back in LA, I visit often and play ball with Austin when he has free time.

But Addison is the Edwards sister who stayed quiet behind the scenes. Even Lex rarely spoke of her, his attention always on Millie, Ava, and Alexa.

She continues to gaze at me with curiosity, allowing me a fleeting moment to observe how much she has changed.

The shape of her face has thinned out slightly, enhancing the pout of her lips. Something within me stirs, this need to rile her up like I'd done when we were kids just to goad some sort of reaction from her.

Finally, she diverts her attention onto the food, prompting me to take a seat across from her.

As I get settled and accept Dad's beer, it's hard to ignore her presence. Across from me, I'm distracted when Cruz steals her food, and the two of them knock into each other playfully. It should come as no surprise since they've been close since they were young kids.

The night is typical of the time spent when in my brother's presence. He's forever acting like an immature dickhead, trying to prove a point like he's the best thing to ever happen to my parents. So, it isn't unusual for him to mouth off. That is until Addison interrupts him and mentions Dad's piercing.

Cruz watches on in horror but not me. I'm amused by such a thing to come out of Miss Innocent's mouth. Of course, Ava is behind this. I make a mental note to speak to her later and ask why the fuck this is talked about amongst the sisters.

But right now, Addison Edwards has a fascination with

Dad, and I won't let this one slide, especially when everyone has stepped out, and it's just her and me.

"So, sorry about the comment, you know, about your dad," she mumbles, unable to look at me.

My eyes are stationed on her. "It appears you're fixated with such novelty."

Addison raises her perfectly shaped eyebrows, followed by a hard smile. "Such novelties don't interest me."

"How would you know unless you've tried?"

"Tried what exactly?" she questions with curiosity.

"Being intimate with a man who can pleasure you in the way you've never experienced before."

Our gazes play a dangerous game, and if I knew what was good for me, I'd turn away right now.

"The world doesn't revolve around sex," she blurts out. "Believe it or not, there are more important and worthy matters which need attention."

I lean against the chair, keeping my lips pressed flat.

"If you say so, Miss Edwards."

"I mean, maybe in your world because you're such a player, that's all you think about. Some of us need more in life."

Who the hell does she think she is? Someone who needs to be shown what a real man can do. And, sweetheart, it's clear *your* world doesn't revolve around sex.

"I can guarantee, Addison, if a man satisfied you, this conversation would never have taken place."

She folds her arms beneath her chest. "You're such an arrogant—"

"Jerk?" I cut her off with a deep stare. "That's how the hate fuck always begins…"

My family walks back in and interrupts our heated conversation. During dessert, my phone buzzes with a text. I quickly glance at the screen.

NICOLE

> Mr. Cooper, are you up for some fun tonight?

I contemplate texting back since Nicole is a guaranteed fuck. But something stops me.

Then, Addison excuses herself to use the bathroom, giving me the perfect getaway.

So, I say goodbye to my parents without bothering to say anything to Cruz.

As for Addison, out of sight, out of mind.

At least, that's what I think on the drive home.

I ignore Nicole's text because something is bothering me. The last thing I need is her coming over and wanting to stay the night like last time.

The bottle of cognac sits on the glass shelf inside my living room. I pour myself a glass then stare outside the large window and into the ocean.

The emerald eyes taunt me, teasing me like a piece of tangled fruit in the middle of a jungle. Her need to voice her opinions of me is something I usually wouldn't fixate on. But tonight, I wasn't conversing with a teenage girl anymore.

Addison Edwards is all woman now.

And one you can't seem to get out of your head.

Inside my pocket is my phone. I pull it out, dialing Ava's number.

"Playboy, what's happening?"

"Did you tell your sisters my dad has a pierced dick?"

"Whoa..." Ava gasps, then continues, "... context, please."

I take a deep breath, walking over to my shelf again to top up my glass. Quickly, I explained to her how it came up over dinner.

"Look, in my defense, it was a long time ago, and I think I heard it from Aunt Adriana."

"You mean everyone knows?"

"I'm pretty sure."

"Jesus Christ, Ava," I mutter, pressing my hand against my forehead as I close my eyes shut for a moment.

"So what? It's your dad. Do you know how much crap I get about my dad?"

"Listen, I'm tired, and it's been a long day."

"Is everything okay? Don't forget you said yes to coming to dinner on Thursday. It's Austin's night off, and if you're a good boy, my husband will cook your favorite lobster."

I chuckle softly. "I better be a good boy then."

We hang up the phone, yet these unwarranted feelings refuse to settle. The cognac eases my racing mind, only slightly.

A restless night is upon me.

And there's only one way to understand what the hell is going through my mind.

I need to see her again, first thing tomorrow morning.

The door swings open to Addison wrapped in a white towel, barely covering her wet body and noticeable dripping hair. The lack of clothing catches me by surprise, doing nothing to ease my curiosity.

As her eyes lay upon me, she draws back, surprised by my visit.

"Do you always answer the door wearing a towel?"

"What are you doing here?" she asks out of breath.

My gaze shifts to the small trickle of blood seeping from her hairline.

"You're bleeding," I say, keeping my focus on her with worry. "What were you doing in the shower?"

She raises her hand to her head then brings it back down to observe the blood on her fingers.

"Shit," she mumbles. "Cruz and his stupid big clown feet."

Her hand clutches onto the top of the towel as she turns around and begins to hop on one foot. Whatever happened, she appears to be in pain.

I step in behind her, but when it's obvious she's struggling, my hands reach beneath her legs to carry her.

"What are you doing?" she shouts in my arms.

She barely weighs anything while I carry her to the kitchen. It's only a short walk and thankfully doesn't give me enough time to focus on how fucking sexy she looks in a towel.

Don't fucking go there.

We reach the countertop to which I carefully set her on. She briefly rests her hand on my shoulder for support, then realizes what she's doing and pulls away.

"Why did you bring me in here?"

I purse my lips, trying to control my frustration since she's so damn stubborn, just like her sisters.

"You're hurt," I remind her, then scour the area to see nothing but boxes. "Do you have a first-aid kit or anything?"

"No," she mumbles. "I'm fine."

Beside the sink is a dishtowel. I lean over to grab it, running it under the faucet to soak it in cold water. When it's damp enough, I turn the water off and bring it to her gash. The moment the cloth touches the small cut, she winces in pain.

"Hold this." I direct her hand to continue holding the cloth against her head. "Is it your foot or ankle hurting?"

Addison remains quiet before letting out a huff. "My ankle, okay? Since when did you turn doctor?"

"Since I completed a first-aid course as part of my role in the company."

"Oh," she mouths softly.

My hands run down her leg against her smooth skin until I reach her ankle. I'm unable to look her in the eye, trying to control how the warmth of her skin is stirring my dick and making me hard. *Jesus Christ, this isn't the fucking time.*

"I'm going to move your ankle slowly and press in a few places," I inform her. "I want you to tell me if it hurts, okay?"

She nods, watching me while scrunching her face.

I remember my training, slowly twisting her foot while watching her expression.

"Does that hurt?"

"No."

Slowly, I turn her foot in the opposite direction.

"How about that?"

"Just a little bit," she admits.

"Okay, well, the good news is the chances are of it being broken are very slim. If you're able to walk and move it, it's most likely you just rolled it.

"Great," she complains, letting go of the cloth. "And on my first day of work."

My gaze is fixated on her face with the way she parts her lips every so often to the blush in her cheeks. I'm sure she's highly aware of the fact she's only wearing a towel as she continues to clutch onto it as if her life depends on it.

Slowly, her head rises, and our eyes lock. This urge to reach out and run my thumb along her bottom lip is too much to bear, but thankfully, there's a knock on the door to break the momentary tension.

"Were you expecting someone?" I question with a head tilt and smirk. "It's early. I didn't interrupt a booty call, did I?"

Addison tries to hop off the counter, grabbing my arm for support.

"It's our delivery. Look, I should get changed. Can you please let them in?"

"Sure."

As she begins to hobble to her room, she briefly turns around. "For the record, I'm not a booty-call person. Perhaps, Mr. Cooper, you're confusing me for yourself."

She disappears, only for the knock to be louder this time. I let the guys in and allow them to bring in the white goods and a couch. There are four of them, and by the time Addison walks back into the room, they're already gone.

As much I prefer her in a towel only, she looks damn fine in her black skirt and white blouse. I've never seen her in corporate wear, and the image of her on her knees sucking on my cock is too hard to resist. Her hair is tied up into a tight bun, away from her face, but a ponytail would've fit the fantasy just right.

"Okay, so you want to explain why you're here?"

Only now, I notice she's carrying her heels. Surely, she can't expect to wear them after her fall.

"You should lay off the high heels for a few days," I scold her.

"How about you answer my question?"

I shake my head, then clear my throat. "I needed to speak to my brother about something."

"You needed to speak to your brother?" she repeats with an amused expression. "He's at training, which I'm sure you knew."

"No, I didn't know."

"Okay, so what's it about?" she pushes.

"It's private."

"Private? Now, I know you're lying," she says with confidence. "If you're here to see me, just admit it."

Her forwardness catches me off guard.

"Why would I want to see you?"

She shrugs her shoulders then turns to make herself a

coffee. When she turns back around, it's with a steaming cup in hand.

"I don't know. You seem to have some sort of fascination with me."

This time, I fold my arms beneath my chest. "Is that so?"

Her lips blow against the steam, then carefully, she takes a sip from the mug. The stare on her face fixates on me blankly, making it challenging to understand where she's going with this.

"I'd love to hang around and chat, but it's the first day of work," she deadpans. "Oh, and your mom insisted I read the book which is your number one bestseller. I'll give credit where credit is due, it was entertaining, and this is why I'm tired."

For a moment, it doesn't drop. Our number one bestseller is a romance book. Then, I remember exactly which one. The one when the male lead is fascinated with eating the girl out everywhere.

And here I thought Miss Edwards was so *innocent*.

I bet, and if only I knew for certain, she played with her sweet pussy from reading the story.

"I've read the book."

Her lashes fly high as her eyes widen. "You've read this book?"

"When a book is a bestseller making the company you work for quite wealthy, you want to know exactly what's inside."

"I guess it makes sense," she mutters, dropping her head quickly. "It doesn't seem like your type of book."

My head cocks to the side. "And what type of books should I be reading?"

"I don't know, more masculine books."

"A rather sexist comment, don't you think?"

A soft sigh passes through her lips.

"You're right. I shouldn't assume a man such as yourself is incapable of reading a romance story," she states rather confidently while straightening her shoulders. "So, did you enjoy it?"

"It was expected of the genre."

"Is that a no?"

"It was interesting," I simply state.

"How so?"

Addison is persistent with finding out just what I think. So, if she wants the truth, I won't hold back.

"The author went into a great deal describing how many times the character would pleasure herself because she was too stubborn to give in to the man she desired."

Addison's expression stiffens, then, with a slight nod, she purses her lips.

"I agree..."

The corner of my mouth slowly rises into a smirk as her body language changes, and she appears to be uncomfortable.

"It makes you wonder what would've happened if she gave into him at the beginning, save herself all the heartache," I whisper, taking a step closer to her.

She takes a step back then finds herself against the counter with no space to move. I'm only inches away with easy access to take her if I want.

And doesn't she look fucking delicious all wide-eyed and shy all of a sudden?

"Well," she mouths softly. "The wait was worth it, in my opinion. The elevator scene was quite explosive."

I nod, drawing back. "Universal fantasy."

"Excuse me?"

"Universal fantasies, surely this comes up when you study psych?"

"I... I need to finish getting ready."

Without another word, she slides past me and almost

bolts to her room. I wait in the kitchen, wishing I could relieve my dick which refuses to fucking soften. My piercing rubs against my boxers, making the sensations all the more heightened.

Addison returns ten minutes later. It's a long time for someone who has already dressed aside from her shoes. She's wearing a pair of flats, but more noticeably, her face appears flushed.

"Finished?"

"Um, yes."

I nod but then grab her hand to bring her fingers toward my nose, just like a scene from the book. The smell of her arousal is all over them, instantly making me want to fuck her right here, right now. She's unable to look me in the eye, but her chest is rising and falling at a fast pace, and I know my actions are affecting her.

"I meant, have you finished making yourself—"

The front door makes a loud sound as my brother yells through the apartment. Quickly, I pull back yet still with an anchored gaze.

Cruz enters the kitchen and stops mid-step. "Oh, hey, what the fuck are you doing here?"

"I was here to see you," I simply say.

"Me? What the hell for?"

Addison clears her throat, still unable to look at me. "I better head out. Don't want to be late on my first day."

Cruz wraps his arms around her, squeezing her tight. I observe this with a slight pang hitting my chest, unsure of what the fuck it was.

"Good luck, Addy. You'll kill it. You tell them crazies, life will be just fine."

Addison pinches his arm with a fierce stare. "Don't make fun of mental illness."

Sitting on the bench is her black purse. She grabs it,

placing it over her shoulder. Then, she lifts her eyes to meet mine.

"Nice to see you again, Masen," she says with a straight face. "The pleasure has been all mine."

And then, she turns away and walks to the door, closing it behind her.

Well, fuck me.

She came.

SEVEN

ADDISON

This isn't how I envisioned my first day on a new job to start.

What the hell was I thinking?

The problem is, I'm *not* thinking every time Masen is around.

I can't seem to control my emotions or even breathe for a moment to think rationally. There's always something about his presence—the unwavering stare to his words that goad some sort of reaction from me, just like when we were kids.

I tried hard to be patient and not feed into bullying, but this time is different between us.

He's a man. A very handsome man if I dare say the truth.

And I guess, well, I am me.

What was I thinking with that whole touch myself while he waited for me in the kitchen? That's right, once again, no control over my thoughts.

The conversation around the book was the tip of an already wet iceberg. Combine the discussion about a female character pleasuring herself and being vulnerable in a towel that barely covered my body, something had to give.

. . .

As he backs me against the countertop, I'm too close to doing something I'll regret later. To make it even worse, with a known playboy who seduces women on a daily basis. I'm just another woman to him, no one special like a deer in the woods, easy to target while hunting.

There's no choice but to leave. I make it to the bedroom unable to understand why my body is betraying me. My skin tingles all over, making it hypersensitive.

Just do it, the voices urge.

It starts innocently, a brush against my swollen clit. I'm unprepared for how my body reacts, desperate for more. It's only a few strokes with my eyes closed and mouth shut to suppress my moans, for the rush of bliss to spread all over me.

My breathing is uneven, as my throat is parched. I give myself a moment, then quickly fix my skirt feeling more in control.

Then, I head back to the kitchen.

The second his eyes feast on me, his expression quickly changes. His signature smirk graces his face like he has some sort of instinct as to what I had just done.

"Finished?"

I clear my throat. "Um, yes."

Then, just like out of the book, he grabs my fingers to inhale my skin. Surely, there's no scent.

I'm proven wrong.

His body tenses, and for a brief moment, he closes his eyes, then they snap open.

"I meant, have you finished making yourself—"

The door makes a loud sound. Cruz's timing is impeccable as always. It's my only chance to escape before doing something else stupid.

"Nice to see you again, Masen," I say with a straight face. "The pleasure has been all mine."

Inside the foyer, I shove a granola bar I'd purchased at a snack stand into my mouth for breakfast. Before entering the elevator, I remove my flats and replace them with a pair of heels, ignoring Masen for telling me I shouldn't wear them. I opt for the ones with the ankle straps, just for a little bit more support. At least I look professional.

I'm still exhausted from no sleep, now on my second cup of coffee as I exit on the fifth floor.

A dark-haired woman is sitting behind the reception desk, dressed nicely in a gray pantsuit. When her eyes fall upon me, she stands up with a warm smile.

"You must be Addison."

"Yes," I respond while extending my hand to shake hers. "Here for my first day."

"I'm Elizabeth but call me Lizzie. I work in reception," she tells me at the same time while motioning for me to follow her. "So, let's get you set up. There are back-to-back appointments today, and Dr. Jenner is quite busy. She's already with a patient."

"So early?"

"It's Beverly Hills. Money makes people screwed-up twenty-four seven."

Lizzie, as she prefers to be called, begins my induction. Everything from a tour of the offices to how to use the coffee machine, and where to find the extra paper for a very temperamental printer.

Since I'm only here part-time, I still have a small desk by the window with a view. It's nothing special, but a desk to call my own.

There are six people who work in the office, so my

primary role is to support the team where needed. Already sitting on my desk is a pile of paperwork. Christine, the lady from accounting, spends an hour with me going through some processes.

By the time lunchtime rolls around, I'm starving. Lizzie offers to take me downstairs to the café to grab a sandwich.

"So, what's your deal?"

I tilt my head in confusion. "My deal?"

"You know, single, assuming not married since no ring on the finger," she says quickly.

"Single and not married. Still trying to finish my degree. That's about it."

Lizzie offers to pay for our lunch, despite me refusing. She pushes my hand, which is carrying my card, out of the way. "On the company. Dr. Jenner is generous with her employees."

I thank her but make a mental note to say thank you to Dr. Jenner when I finally get a chance to sit with her.

"Um, so, aren't you the daughter of Lex Edwards?" Lizzie asks, almost dragging it out like it's some secret.

"Yes, one of his daughters."

Lizzie's eyes bulge as she bites into her turkey sandwich. "Your life must be amazing, not boring like you're making it out to be."

A small laugh escapes me. "I have a great family, but trust me, there's really nothing interesting going on with me."

Then, the flashback occurs to this morning.

I take a deep breath, wishing to get off the topic of my so-called uneventful life.

Lizzie is quick to inform me about her life as a single mum with a five-year-old daughter. Apparently, the father is absent. Some ex who bailed when he found out about the pregnancy.

"So, basically, I don't date. Therefore, don't have sex."

"That's a lot to take in," I say slowly, mid-chew. "But I understand the whole dating thing, especially since any potential partner can lead to being a stepfather to your daughter."

"Kacey is her name," Lizzie mentions with a smile. "I mean, sometimes it would be nice just to have a man worship me, sexually, that is."

I nod with a chuckle. "A girl's gotta eat. Is that the saying?"

Lizzie tilts her head back, laughing with me. "Amen."

After lunch, the waiting room is nonstop with patients. I manage to make myself a quick coffee, my third for the day. This time, I add an extra shot of caffeine just to make it through.

Lizzie wheels her chair over to me. She brings a bunch of files with her, all of which need data entry. Thankfully, I can type quickly, and my accuracy skills are pretty high.

Dr. Jenner is still consulting with a patient who seems to take longer than an hour. I want to ask Lizzie what's going on but decide against it. It's only my first day, and I shouldn't be judging patients who need more than an hour to talk about their problems.

With a pile of files in my hand, I walk outside to the main reception area to return them to Lizzie when I see a familiar pose sitting inside the waiting room. The perfectly tailored black Gucci suit, with tanned leather shoes, belongs to the one and only Eric Kennedy.

"OMG," he almost shouts. "Addy, is this your new job? I had no idea."

Eric presses his hand to his neck like it's the biggest news of the week. I knew this wasn't the case when, according to Millie, Rocky and Nikki were busted having sex in an airplane restroom.

"Yes, this is the new job that I was talking about. Surely, Mom would've told you?"

"Your mother says a lot of things, all of which goes in one ear and out the other, unless, of course, she's talking about your father in the bedroom."

I press my lips into a firm smile. "My mother would never reveal my father's secrets to anyone. I know her well."

"Touché, young grasshopper."

"Anyway, what are you doing here?"

"I'll have you know I come here every week," he states matter-of-factly. "To air my grievances. It's important to get it out of my system, so I can enjoy the weekend."

I walk closer to him, so Lizzie can't hear me.

"So let me get this straight. You pay one of the top therapists in Beverly Hills to air your grievances every week?"

Eric crosses his arms beneath his chest, then nods.

"Don't you air your grievances enough between Mom, Adriana, and what about Kate?"

"Fine," he answers in a disgruntled tone. "There are some issues in the bedroom."

My hand raises to stop him from speaking any further.

"You're right," I tell him, "Dr. Jenner is the perfect person to speak to."

Dr. Jenner exits the room and comes over to say hello.

"I'm so sorry, Addison. It's been quite a day," she says, catching her breath. "Have you settled in okay?"

"Yes," I respond with a warm smile. "Lizzie and Christine have been accommodating by showing me around and training me on processes."

"I'm glad." She glances toward Eric. "Mr. Kennedy, it's nice to see you again."

"Oh, cut the crap, Josephine. You saw me last night drunk at that gay bar wearing only my boxers and fake mustache, which looks like it belonged to a porno star from the eighties."

Dr. Jenner flattens her lips, keeping her expression at bay. "And some sight that was, Eric. Now, shall we?"

Just like the other patient, Eric goes well over the hour. By the time he exits the room, he does look refreshed with a glowing face.

"All done," he says cheerfully.

"What are your plans for this weekend?"

"Well, for starters, I'll be avoiding Tristan's mother because she's in town." He rolls his eyes with an overdramatic sigh. "I've also got a few events, ready to break out my new Prada loafers."

"Exciting."

"And you? Do you have anything you want to share?"

My posture turns rigid at the same time I unknowingly suck in my cheeks. The paranoia gets the better of me, worried he can read my thoughts like some broody vampire, and this morning's dirty secret will be revealed.

"Uh, me, why would you say that?"

"Lighten up, doll. It was just a question."

I draw in a breath followed by a smile. "You know me, Daddy's favorite. Nothing at all is happening with me."

Eric laughs, then pats me on the shoulder. "Yes, indeed, Daddy's favorite. You're definitely not Millie with her age-gap romance."

"Most definitely not, no billionaires in my bedroom."

"And you're not Ava with her forbidden pregnancy," he continues with a proud grin.

"You're the perfect little daughter."

"That's probably going a little bit too far. I mean, I'm not the perfect little daughter.

I can have fun."

A rude snort escapes Eric's mouth. "Oh really? Come on, Addy. Tell me the last time you actually had fun."

My hands cross beneath my chest with a darting gaze.

"First of all, my idea of fun and your idea of fun are two very different things."

"Addy, sweetheart," he murmurs while touching my cheek with the back of his hand.

"You've got to live a little. You're twenty-four with a stunning body. The body of, well, a twenty-four-year-old. Men want to be with you, and men want to be inside you. Studying is important, so is having fun."

If only he knew about this morning, the so-called fun, or shall we call it 'the thrill of making myself come in less than one minute because of a man I loathe.' A man who stood outside waiting then had the audacity to smell my fingers for his own satisfaction.

"Eric, everyone is concerned about me because I don't have a boyfriend, and I don't like to date," I pause momentarily, then catch my breath. "I promise you I'm fine. If I need to get laid, I'll go get laid. Do I think that's healthy? No, I don't think one-night stands are healthy at all."

Eric pinches the bridge of his nose while closing his eyes briefly.

"Don't stress me out, woman. I've just aired my grievances, and now you want to argue with me about one-night stands?"

"Please give me one reason on how they're healthy?"

"If he's got a small wang, you never have to see it again," Eric blurts out.

I lower my head to suppress my laughter but fail miserably.

"Okay, I'm going to give you that. I can't say I've ever experienced a really small one, so perhaps my opinion is skewed."

Eric moves in closer. "Who are we talking about and what size? Because once, it was so small, I didn't even realize it was in and just got up and left the room."

I shake my head in disgust, wondering how we got here, all from an anything-exciting- this-weekend friendly chat.

"Eric, I'm at work. This isn't the time to talk about my sexual conquest or perhaps lack thereof," I gently scold him. "But when things start getting hot with some man—"

"I'll be the first to know?" he asks, too eagerly.

"Sure. Along with Millie, Ava, Luna, Alexa, Jessa, and everybody else who insists on knowing all about my personal life."

"I smell sarcasm," he sneers.

I grab both his hands with a grin. "Smart little boy."

The workday goes longer than expected, so by the time I reach the apartment, I'm utterly exhausted.

My heels come off before I even make it to the front door. As I carry them in one hand, I rummage through my purse for the keys.

Upon opening the door, Cruz is sitting on the couch playing a game on the television.

The boxes are put away, leaving the living room looking clean and organized.

"Hey, Addy, what's up?" he greets, but his eyes are focused on the screen. "How was your first day?"

I let out a groan, throwing my shoes onto the floor and plonking myself on the couch. Every part of me aches like I've run a marathon. I want nothing more than to fall asleep, but I opt for resting my head on the small velvet teal cushion. Then, I realize I'm sitting on the new couch.

"So, everything arrived?"

Cruz turns his head with a frown. "Um, yeah, you were here this morning to accept the delivery, remember?"

And we're back to this morning.

It's all a blur. At least the essential parts are a blur.

"Sorry, it's been a long day." I yawn, too tired even to cover my mouth politely. "Have you eaten?"

"Yeah, earlier when I was with the guys after training. But I'm down for some curry from downstairs."

"You order, and I'm gonna take a shower."

As I walk toward the bedroom to grab my PJs, Cruz shouts my name from the living room.

"How hot do you want it?

"Not burn-my-asshole hot like last time," I yell back.

Cruz laughs. "Both our assholes were burning from memory."

Inside my room, the memory of this morning flashes before my eyes. I shake my head, willing my mind to detour to something else. Shower, just take a shower, and the world will feel right again.

The warm water eases my tense muscles, and for a brief moment, I accidentally fall asleep while standing. I awaken when I bump into the wall, still covered in shampoo.

It almost becomes too exhausting even to get out. Finally, I manage only because Cruz yells at the door. The food has arrived. *Damn, how long was I in there for?*

The curry tastes extra fantastic tonight. After my second bowl, I continue to pick at the naan bread while making myself comfy on the sofa. Cruz finishes the remaining food then focuses back on his game.

"I'm just gonna lay here next to you and rest my eyes," I tell him with another yawn following.

"I look forward to your snores."

I kick him gently. "I don't snore, you goof."

Slowly, I begin to doze off. Then, my phone beside me pings with a text notification. I swear to God my sisters are relentless. How they get anything done is beyond me.

My eyes gaze at the screen sleepily, but the unknown number catches my attention.

UNKNOWN

> So, we didn't finish our conversation this morning.

Suddenly, I'm wide awake. My eyes are no longer bleary-eyed, assuming this is Masen. Who else would've texted me this about this morning?

ME

> How did you get my number?

MASEN

> I have my ways. Does it bother you?

ME

> It doesn't bother me. It's just we never talk. I'm not Ava.

MASEN

> I'm glad you're not Ava because I swear your sister could talk about absolutely nonsense and still make a drama out of it.

My lips press together to hold back my laughter. Then, I type back quickly with a burst of energy keeping me wide awake.

ME

> For once, we agree on something, but we don't exactly talk like I said.

MASEN

> Funny that because we talked last night. In fact, you had a lot to say about my father's member.

ME

> You did not just say member.

MASEN

I'm trying to refrain from using words that would be deemed offensive, especially to a lady like yourself.

ME

I'm not sure whether to be offended or say thank you.

MASEN

So about this morning…

ME

There's nothing to say besides thank you. I guess I could've been really hurt if you weren't here. And, you know, do something extra stupid like wear heels to work.

MASEN

That's not what I'm talking about.

I let out a heavy sigh, but then Cruz turns his head to glance at me.

"I thought you were tired?"

"Oh yeah," I mumble. "I just wanted to catch up on my texts because I didn't have a chance today."

He doesn't ask anything else, switching his focus again.

I quickly type back, unsure as to why, since it's clear Masen wants to discuss what happened this morning. All of a sudden, I'm embarrassed by my actions. The key to moving on and making sure it never happens again is to discuss it then close the book on the matter.

ME

What do you want me to say?

MASEN

Nothing you don't want to say, Addison. But perhaps there's something I have that you want.

ME

And what is that, Mr. Cooper?

I'm half-expecting him to say something dirty. As someone who doesn't know how to dirty talk, I prepare myself for what he's about to say, taking a deep breath as I wait in anticipation. Luckily, Cruz is oblivious.

MASEN

I have part two of the book, which riled some sort of reaction from you. That's if you have finished part one. I won't give away any spoilers.

His text catches my attention. I'm certain Presley said the book isn't out yet, supposed to be released in two months. It's no surprise he has a copy, but after today, I'd forgotten all about it. From memory, I'm more than halfway through the book.

ME

Fine, I'll finish it tonight. I'm not sure if I'll need book two since romance isn't really my thing.

MASEN

I'll just wait for your desperate text when you're done.

Arrogant jerk.

I tell Cruz I'm heading to bed, to which he offers to clean up.

After brushing my teeth, I climb into bed and open my Kindle app to continue where I left off. I'm eager to prove the jerk is wrong. There's not a ton to the plot. The couple is screwing each other all over Manhattan—bars, elevators, and restaurants.

Okay, so technically, they're not having sex yet. Basically, he eats her out wherever and whenever he can, making it some weird obsession.

I'm sitting up in bed with a bottle of water, hoping the Indian food doesn't do a number on my stomach. But, as I continue to read on, the plot thickens. The story gets juicier, and this couple is so in love with each other but just can't get it right. So, instead, they do what they do best—fuck each other like tomorrow doesn't exist.

It's nothing but the thrill of the chase, the possibility of getting caught. Each time they're intimate with each other, they just don't realize how deeply they're falling in love.

But more prominently, how hard it is to pull themselves out of this tangled web they've found themselves in.

It's two in the morning when I finish. Thankfully, I'm not working today, just studying. I try to fall asleep with my lamp off, but I can't get this ending out of my mind. The way they spiraled out of control and how their desires drove them apart in the end.

The book left me with no answers and a goddamn cliffhanger.

I *hate* that he's right. But he does have something I want.

Masen Cooper is dangling the shiny red apple.

And I can already taste just how delicious it will be.

EIGHT

MASEN

"Excuse me, sir. Another drink?" My eyes are fixated on the cluster of clouds as I stare out the window of the plane. The hostess waits with an annoying smile, but I don't even look her way. Been there, done *that*.

"No, thank you."

In front of me is my laptop with a spreadsheet on the screen. Usually, I try to catch up on work while on a flight since they're always tedious and mind-numbing.

But not this time.

The trip to Dallas was quick and uneventful. All work and absolutely no play. However, this time, it was my doing. I just wasn't in the mood. So, I did my best to stay away from people in general because my short temper and lack of patience grew thin during this trip.

It suited me just fine. It's the life I've always led—a life of solitary.

This life I chose for myself has never been a concern to anyone, even my parents. I'm not a relationship guy, nor do I ever see myself committing to anyone. The longest relationship I've had is a month, and even then, I grew bored of the woman the moment she wanted more.

I've watched my parents my entire life, seen how two very different personalities and people come together each day, lovingly. My dad has his moments, but the man is under some goddamn spell when it comes to Mom. She truly is the leader of our family, not that anyone of us cares. The woman is a queen, and I'll give credit where credit is due. She manages to tolerate all of us men and still shows up to a stressful job.

But this life I lead, there's nothing wrong with it. I get what I want when I want it. And just because I'm thinking about *Addison* doesn't mean anything.

Nothing at all.

All day yesterday, I distracted myself with work, never thinking twice about our encounter that morning. Okay, so her scent is engrained in my memory, tormenting me, but if I wanted to, I could've fucked someone else to get rid of the pestering thoughts. It seemed like too much effort, so I did my best to ignore it.

Yet, despite my reluctance to think about her throughout the day, the signs were everywhere.

It started with Ava and her not-so-subtle reminder about dinner tomorrow night. She even went on and on about the lobster, which was difficult to ignore. Austin is a great cook, and it's been a while since I ate his specialty. In the end, I told her to stop bugging me, I'll be there, and that's that.

Then, the host of the convention I attended last minute was conveniently named Addison. Again, trivial things but nevertheless a constant reminder.

It didn't stop there.

It was a late evening last night when Mom called to inform me that the sequel to our bestselling novel was completed. Normally, I don't get involved during the process of any manuscripts being reviewed at the early stages. Yet, this novel is bestselling worldwide. The revenue, and interest, are beyond anything we've ever seen. Only a few hours ago, we were contacted by a big production company to write a screenplay to bring it to film.

The pre-orders on the sequel have already exceeded our expectations. So, it's imperative this book hits the reader's expectations.

Mom mentioned the book is ready to go to beta readers, a group of young and older women whose opinions and feedback is what the author and Mom's editorial team look for.

But I knew who the perfect person would be to give their opinion. The person who enjoyed the book enough to take note from it then touched herself inside her bedroom while I waited patiently outside.

"The pleasure is all mine..."

So, I caved, sending her a text but not without drinking two glasses of bourbon to talk myself out of it. I wanted to talk about yesterday morning, and if it weren't for my idiotic brother interrupting us, perhaps there would've been a different outcome.

An outcome that plays in my head like a sick fantasy. How sweet the innocent Addison Edwards will taste with my tongue buried between her legs as she begs me to make her come.

The pilot announces our descent, and within an hour and a half, I'm back inside my office—no rest for the wicked. By the late afternoon, I'm barely managing to control my anger. It's another exhausting day of incompetent idiots trying to prove they deserve a pay raise for their efforts.

I've been staring at the spreadsheet again for a solid hour, trying to understand how employees who have degrees in accounting are giving me numbers that make absolutely no sense.

I hear the click of heels and the familiar pace that belongs to my mother down the hall. There's a soft knock on the door though she walks in anyway.

"Your father has just flown to San Francisco. I'll be joining him tomorrow," Mom informs me while typing something quickly on her phone.

"Do you need me to fly up for this meeting as well?"

"No, you stay here." I hear the exhaustion in her voice. "You manage these people better than your father. His patience is wearing incredibly thin."

"And so is mine, dear mother."

"Masen," she murmurs, glancing at me with her typical concerned face. "I always say this to your father, and I'll say this to you again. You must learn to control your temper. I understand that things don't always work out the way you think they should, but everyone is fighting their own battles, ones we may not know about."

I tilt my head to the left, then the right, cracking my neck to alleviate the pressure.

"When people are employed with our company, I don't care about their battles. They're paid to work for us. End of story."

Mom lets out a heavy sigh. "I didn't raise you to be that type of boy, Masen."

"Man, mother, not boy," I correct her but soften my tone since my arrogance is upsetting her. "Just in case you're forgetting."

"Of course," she continues with a smile. "A man who bailed early for a booty call the other night."

I press my lips together flatly. "Right, yeah, I forgot."

We speak for a little while longer before she leaves, but not without reminding me about an event on Saturday night. It's for charity, and just before she steps out, she leaves a not-so-subtle reminder to bring a date.

The office is deserted tonight, and everyone leaves for the day except the janitors doing their job. My phone continues to ping with notifications, but I choose to ignore them since they weren't who I was expecting.

Why the fuck does this bother me so much?

Masen Cooper doesn't chase after women, nor do I beg for anything. Surely, it's just my ego taking a massive hit right now.

I swivel my chair to stand up, moving toward the large window. The sun is setting in the distance as I watch from my office. My frustration over my unfocused headspace disappears, if only for a moment. Then, a sound catches my attention. I assume it's the janitors, so I don't bother to turn around until the sound is of a throat clearing.

My shoulders turn with my head following only to see Addison standing at the door. The sight of her stirs this unknown feeling, something I can't decipher. I'm surprised, or more so curious as to why she's paying me a visit.

It mustn't be a workday as she's wearing a white halter dress that sits mid-thigh. My gaze falls toward her feet, admiring the tan sandals she wears and her long, lean legs. But slowly, they drag up until our eyes meet, my own burning with curiosity.

"To what do I owe the pleasure?" I ask, crossing my arms with a wide smirk.

She pretends to come off annoyed, but there's always something behind her quiet exterior which remains a mystery.

"Turns out you do have something I want," she says with her emerald eyes fixated on me.

My head cocks to the side. "And exactly what's that?"

She moves slowly toward my desk, placing her hands on the desktop. Quietly, she scans the area, which only has a few papers since I prefer to have things in order.

"I need part two," she states, pulling back with a frustrated sigh.

"I see." The manuscript is inside my drawer to keep it confidential from prying eyes. I pull the top drawer out, retrieve it, then place it on my desk. "I thought Miss Edwards didn't do romance?"

"It's not just about the romance," she mumbles.

"Oh?" I question, moving closer to her. "What else about the story is it you enjoy?"

My eyes are drawn to the goosebumps forming across her delicate skin. The room is quiet aside from the humming sound of the AC running.

But, as I listen attentively, the soft breaths escaping her lips are like music to my ears. She's nervous, maybe even anxious like prey being watched by the hunter.

"The power," she responds with sudden confidence.

I pause momentarily, tilting my head again with slight confusion. "The power?"

Her back is still facing me, yet I step closer, trapping her body where she stands. Slowly, I brush my finger against her exposed shoulder and move her hair to observe her skin better.

"The author makes us believe the male protagonist insists on tasting her at his command." Her reflection in the window shows me her eyes are closed as she speaks. The blood pumps hard throughout me, but the focus is on my hard cock, which I press against her ass without even thinking. "But it is she who holds power."

"So, tell me, Miss Edwards," I whisper against her ear,

pressing harder, waiting for her to tell me to stop. "Who has the power now?"

"Me," she murmurs.

"Is that so?"

Addison moves her hand on top of mine, then gradually turns her body, so our eyes meet. Her stare is full of lust, and fire burns in her eyes while she bites her lip so teasingly.

"I know, you want to taste me. Actually, I'm sure begging isn't off the agenda," she says, still focused on my unwavering gaze. "But perhaps we can come to some sort of an agreement."

A smirk plays on my lips. "An agreement?"

"Neither one of us is looking for commitment. So, I propose a one-time thing."

My hand trails her cheekbone and slides down her neck, finding itself flat against the middle of her exposed chest. Just one move to the left or right, and I'll have her in my hands. Her perfect tits are calling out to me, but I play it safe for now and glide my hand down to rest on her thigh.

"And what happens during this one-time thing?"

It's Addison's turn to touch me, running her index finger along my bottom lip. Unknowingly, she bites her bottom lip again.

"I want you to taste me."

I'm done waiting, slamming my lips onto hers with a feverish passion. She tastes so fucking perfect, like strawberries mixed with honey. My tongue battles with hers as she moans into our kiss, but then she pulls away out of breath.

Her emerald eyes anchor mine, leaving my heart to beat erratically from just one fucking kiss.

"I didn't mean my mouth." She breathes steadily while reaching for my hand and sliding it between her thighs. "I meant here."

Fuck. Me.

She wants me to eat her pussy, and that's that.

I keep my thoughts to myself, quietly moving my fingers beneath her panties. I thrust my fingers into her, groaning as they slide so effortlessly. Careless in my actions, I keep finger-fucking, relishing in how soaked her pussy becomes around my fingers while fighting the urge not to spread her on my desk and fuck her right now.

Inside my pants, I'm ready to fucking blow. All this control I had, perhaps I'm wrong. I'm tormenting myself just as much, and Addison Edwards is all I can think about tasting right now.

With her chest heaving, and her body wriggling from the intensity, I sense her impending orgasm but pull my fingers out just in time. Raising them to her lips, I watch her taste her own juices before running my tongue along her mouth and tasting her arousal.

"Sweet," I murmur, our gaze locking into each other. "But I want more."

Both my hands wrap around her ass to lift her and spread her on my desk. I push her ankles apart, observing her soaked white panties right in front of me. She's the devil in disguise, pure and innocent, begging me to make her sweet pussy come.

I want nothing more than to see her climax at this moment, but I take my time, teasing her while running my tongue around her clit. Her scent is driving me insane as the tip of my tongue is hovering around her sensitive spot.

Suddenly, she places her hands around my head. "Make me come, now."

With force, she pushes my face forward, and my tongue sucks at her clit so readily. Against the table, she arches her back and tries to suppress her moans. I slide my finger inside her again, taking it slow until she doesn't complain, so I slide in a second finger.

This time, she gasps.

Her body tenses, the grip on my shoulders tightens. "Please don't stop... I'm just about to..."

With one last flick of my tongue, I feel her contract all over my fingers which causes me to blow inside my boxers. *Shit.*

The heavy pants begin to quiet down, so I remove my fingers slowly. As I stand up, watching her lay in front of me like a goddess demanding I worship her, I bring my fingers up to my lips and taste her again.

Perfect.

I try to ignore the stickiness inside my boxers, extending my hand to pull her up. Addison purposely shifts her gaze to the hem of her dress, pulling it down quietly. I bring my hand to her chin, lifting it so our eyes meet.

"The proposal is a two-time thing," I say while staring calmly into her eyes. "And the next time you see me, I expect you to return the favor, Miss Edwards."

A small smile plays on her lips. "Deal, Mr. Cooper."

NINE

ADDISON

The door slams behind me as I lean against it out of breath.

My body is on fire, a shade of pink from the heat crawling on my skin. I'm unable to move from this spot, my feet and legs refusing to work together as I rely on the door to keep me upright.

What the hell did I just do?

Something is lodged inside my throat, making it hard to swallow and breathe. In a panic, I race to the kitchen and grab a glass of water to cool myself down with the hope of returning to the normal temperature. After two drinks, my body slowly begins to relax, but then the flashback hits me like thunder in the night.

"I want you to taste me."

My eyes shut tight while I shake my head, trying to rid myself of the memory. Masen's eyes find me, taunting me with his sexy stare as if I belong to him like a prized possession.

The moment I arrived at the office and saw him standing next to the window, something took over me. The ordinarily quiet me was locked in a cell and running the show was the woman who wanted to know what a forbidden moment felt like.

It felt like nothing I'd ever experienced.

There was a rush, this intensity which made me say and do things with desperation. What I'd asked of him, I'd never asked a man before.

And in return, my body fell captive to his very skilled *tongue*.

The familiar tingle starts to spread all over me again, forcing me to open my eyes and face reality. I'm home, away from him. Once I shower and get settled, all will be forgotten.

I jump into the shower and allow the hot water to rain over me. But, as I stand here naked, my hands wander to my breasts. My nipples stand erect, sensitive with every touch and glide of the soap. I don't understand why my body doesn't calm itself down, given the intensity of tonight.

It's almost like it wants more.

My thoughts are dangerous, so I turn the faucet to cold and let the water wash over me until I can't handle the temperature.

Back in my room, I change into a tee and shorts. As I sit on my bed, I realize there's nothing for me to do to occupy my mind. My paper is done, along with the reading required for next week's classes. I guess I can stream something to watch, but I'm not really in the mood.

I should be tired, yet I'm wide awake.

My phone is beside me, so I pick it up and open my social media. I spend a few minutes scrolling aimlessly, but curiosity gets the better of me. Inside the search function, I type Masen's name. Nothing comes up linked to him, just a few Mason Coopers with the spelling of the first name different.

Then, I decide to take it to the next step. I google him.

There are several images of him with random women, some even wearing bikinis. The photos are in nightclubs, beach clubs, and restaurants. A burning sensation spreads across my stomach, prompting me to stop looking at the images. Fact, the man is sexy.

But I've just played with the player.

Cruz shouts through the apartment, arriving home after classes. He jumps on my bed to sit beside me, bumping my shoulder while I stare at the wall, fidgeting.

"What a fucking day," he says, exasperated. "Coach grilled me about a few of my moves. Then he started talking about my out-of-state opportunities."

My mind wanders again, the flashes of *him* between my legs with a tortured gaze.

"Why is everyone on my back? I'm over it," Cruz complains furthermore.

The two fingers thrust inside me.

"Addy, are you even listening to me? What's up with you?"

"No... nothing's up with me," I stammer, breaking out of my daze. "Why would you think that?"

He shrugs his shoulders. "I don't know. You're acting weird."

"I'm fine."

"Okay then, so what do you want to eat tonight?"

"Eat?"

"Yeah, you know, food?"

I scratch the base of my neck. "I'm not hungry."

"Then I guess I'll just make a sandwich or something," he mumbles.

"You're not going out?"

"Don't feel like it," he mumbles, sliding his body down then turning to the side to face me. "I'd rather stay here with you."

His body moves closer to mine, pressed up against my side, making my skin extra heated. I need to be alone, slightly annoyed he's not out with some chick like he'd have been if he still lived on campus.

"I'm tired, Cruz. I'm pretty much going to crash now."

"It's eight in the evening?"

"Yeah, well, long day," I tell him.

Cruz rolls in the opposite direction with a grunt. "Fine, goodnight, Grandma."

I've done everything to distract myself from last night since sleeping didn't exactly work.

At the crack of dawn, I got up and changed into my running gear. I ran on the pavement beside the beach with my headphones on, playing club music which is just beats and no lyrics.

There were a few other joggers, but nothing too busy until the sun rose, and every person was out walking their dog.

Cruz had already left for training when I got back home, giving me the peace I need. But, of course, a shower is my first priority since I'm drenched in sweat.

I don't have work again until Monday, so I tried to drown myself in studying again since it comes so easily to me, except for today. I'm unable to concentrate, distracted by the way my foot taps so anxiously on the floor.

When I manage to gain some momentum in the late afternoon, my phone rings with Cruz's goofy face flashing on the front. Letting out a huff, I hit accept.

"What?" I answer with an annoyed tone.

"Is that how you greet your roommate and the love of your life?"

The corners of my lips curve upward into a smile. The background sounds are really loud, forcing Cruz to raise his voice for me to hear him.

"Where are you? I can barely hear."

"I'm at a bar," he tells me, the echo of laughter surrounding him. "A couple of the guys wanted to go out for some drinks, and you know how it is."

I know exactly how it is. The boys convince Cruz, who initially says no. But, after much pressure, he finally caves then winds up drunk as hell, with me having to deal with him.

So, there go my plans of studying since he'll probably call me in a few hours to pick him up from some woman's house he ended up with.

"Listen, Addy. I need a huge favor from you."

"What is it now?" I ask, irritated. "If this is about bringing someone home, you know the rules. At least introduce me to her first. That way, I know who stole my wallet in the morning."

"It's about tomorrow night," he begins with but then is distracted by someone yelling his name. "I need you to be my date to this event Mom is making me go to."

I close the screen of my MacBook. "Date? What event is it?"

"Something about charity. Anyway, she asked me to be there. You know I hate going to these things, so I'm not short of begging, just so you know."

My body moves forward as I lean my elbows on the desk.

"Who else is going?"

"I don't know, Addy. I didn't ask because I don't care," he says with frustration. "So, will you be my date?"

"Okay, I'll be your date. Can you at least give me the dress code? This is very last minute."

"Mom said to wear a suit."

"I meant for me, moron."

"Addy, if I have to wear a suit, then I think you need to dress in something fancy. Do you hear me? Fancy not slutty."

A small laugh escapes me. "So protective, like a big brother though technically I'm older than you."

"C'mon, is that how you look at me? What if we're soul-mates, and we have no idea."

This time, my laughter grows louder. "I think you're drunk and need to get laid. I'll see you later."

"Wait, Addy?"

"Yeah?"

"I promise I won't bring anyone home," he assures me, but I sense something odd in his tone.

I'm probably overthinking it because he's had a lot to drink and is unable to control his emotions. Typical Cruz, getting all sentimental after drinking beer and shots.

As soon as I hang up the phone, I jump out of bed and scour through my wardrobe. There's nothing in there remotely formal. It's just a bunch of sundresses and one cock-tail dress, but it borderlines on being more suited to a club scene.

Dammit.

I rack my brain thinking about what dresses were at my parents' house, but certain I'd worn them at too many events to recycle again. Great, now I'm thinking like Ava.

Ava, of course. Mrs. Fashionista will have something I can borrow.

My eyes scan the room for my keys, spotting them on my dresser. I quickly change into a pair of navy sweats, sneakers, and a white midriff sports top. It'll only be Ava and possibly Austin who'll see me anyway.

The drive is only fifteen minutes away. When I arrive, I drive down the side entrance to the back of the house as they have two driveways. I remove the keys from the ignition and find Ava's house key buried in between my apartment keys. There are two keys, one belonging to Ava's place and one to Millie's.

However, I use my key to open the door and enter with caution this time. I've learned my lesson after accidentally seeing Will and Mille half-naked in the kitchen.

"Ava, are you here? I have an emergency," I shout while trying to jiggle my key out of the lock.

Voices are filtering from inside the dining room.

"Addy, is that you?" Ava yells back.

I stop at the kitchen counter to grab a banana from the fruit bowl. Quickly peeling the skin, I take a big bite while looking for my sister.

As I turn the corner into the dining room, I stop dead in my tracks.

"Addy, what are you doing here? Is everything okay?"

My mouth falls open. Then my eyes widen at the sight of Masen sitting at the table beside Austin. He's dressed in a navy suit similar to the one he wore last night when he...

This can't be happening.

I can barely swallow the banana in my mouth, but I'm not in a position to spit it out either. Suddenly, the panic sets in as I begin to hyperventilate. The room is extra warm even though my midriff exposes a lot of skin.

"Aunty Addy," Emmy calls while reaching out for me.

My niece's greeting distracts me enough to swallow the rest of my banana. She squirms out of her chair to run for my legs. I lift her and kiss her cheek even though there's pumpkin all over her face. More and more, she's looking like Austin and less like Ava, aside from the color of her eyes.

Purposely, I avoid looking at Masen, knowing he's staring at me and waiting for attention.

"I needed to speak to you about something urgent, but I didn't realize you have company," I barely manage, praying my skin doesn't turn red from embarrassment. "I'll just go. I can talk to you later."

Ava stands up. "Don't be silly. There's food here."

I raise my hand to decline the offer. "Please, I'm fine. I just ate."

"A banana isn't dinner," Ava points out.

"Actually..." I begin with, then continue quickly, "... bananas contain fiber, potassium, vitamin C, vitamin B6, and several other beneficial plant compounds."

Austin presses his lips together to suppress his smile. "It's true."

"Fine, I'm not arguing with you two again. The avocado argument got me pregnant."

I scrunch up my face. "Too much information, Ava."

"What's the emergency? Man problems?" Ava laughs at herself. "Oh, that's right. Not you, Miss I-don't-need-a-man-for-anything."

My gaze flicks up to meet Masen's devious stare. The left corner of his lip is curled up into a smirk, and I quickly swallow the lump inside my throat and ignore just how handsome he looks sitting across from me.

And how sexy he looked between my legs.

"It's nice to see you again, Addison," Masen says in a sarcastic tone.

I press my lips together into a hard smile. "Well, actually, you saw me at the beginning of the week, remember?"

"How silly of me to forget," he notes in dark amusement. "My apologies, I've been preoccupied at work. There was something important which needed my undivided attention."

The adrenaline shoots through me, causing a tingling sensation in my chest. This is what the arrogant jerk wants, to see me crumble at his words like the timid and shy woman he thinks I am.

But something inside me begins to stir. If he wants to play, I'll play just as dirty.

"I hope you completed the task to satisfaction. There's nothing worse than incompetency inside the office."

Masen's expression remains fixed, but his hazel eyes refuse to look anywhere else.

"I couldn't agree more. There's nothing worse than someone who refuses to do the job right," he chastises. "When you commit to something, you need to give it your best. Never back down. I expect the same in return."

My thighs press together as I quickly turn away and smile at Emmy. Okay, maybe I'm not so good at this so-called game. If Ava and her family weren't here, I'd know exactly what to do with his smug face right now. *Bury it between my legs again.*

"Look, whatever is going on between you two, seriously, it's so not ten years ago anymore," Ava mentions with a frown. "We're all adults. The two of you just need to shake on it and be friends."

"I can be amicable," I tell her.

Ava turns to look at Masen, waiting for a response. "And you?"

"I have no idea what you're talking about, Ava. Your sister and I just never had anything in common, isn't that right?"

I nod. "It's true. I mean, he's a manwhore, and I'm the woman who studies such behavior and will eventually be charging women who need therapy for encountering men just like him."

Austin shakes his head, hiding his grin while Ava bursts out laughing.

"Okay, stay as enemies," Ava resigns. "Whatever works for you two."

Across the table, Masen's sneer is very typical of him. I cross my arms proudly having pointed out the truth.

"Moving on to why I came here. I need to borrow a dress."

Ava's eyes light up. "Please tell me it's a date!"

I shrug my shoulders. "Something like that."

"Please excuse us, gentlemen. We shan't be long."

Ava grabs my arms to follow her outside the room without even warning me. I don't even get a chance to see Masen's reactions, but he wouldn't care anyway. Last night, we agreed for it to be a one-time thing. Okay, so maybe a two-time thing, but that's that.

Inside Ava's room, the wardrobe is massive, of course, and bigger than my entire bedroom in the apartment. Everything is neatly categorized into colors, garments, and even her jewelry is displayed in glass cabinets.

"Okay," she squeals. "Who's the lucky man you're going on a date with?"

My hands run across the different fabrics, stopping at a red gown with a long sash draping from the shoulder.

"It's Cruz. It's not a date. I'm going as his date to some work thing for his parents."

Ava lets out a dramatic groan. "Here I was getting all excited that you were going to get laid."

I continue to sift through the clothes but ignore her comment.

"This was like earlier in the night, when I was trying to set up Masen with this model I know. I mean, she's so his type. He was so blah about it."

My lips flatten, but I can't help myself. "Masen has a type?"

"One word for you, bimbo."

"Oh," I mouth, suddenly feeling like an idiot.

Ava begins to take dresses out for me to try on, but my phone pings in my pocket. I pull it out to read the text.

MASEN

Who are you going on a date with?

I read the question again, wondering why he cares, and quickly type back as Ava is rambling about my so-called perfect breasts.

ME

Does it matter? I'm sure you spend your free time buried in other women.

I wait for his response, but it never comes, so I focus my attention back on Ava. I decide to go for the red of all the dresses she pulls out.

We head back to the dining room, but Masen is nowhere to be seen.

"Masen had to leave. Something urgent came up," Austin tells us.

"A vagina?" Ava muses, followed by a laugh. "That boy, honestly."

"Leave him alone, he's single, and he doesn't need judgment from the women in his life."

"Fine," Ava complains, then licks her lips while rubbing her belly. "More food for me."

Ten minutes later, I say goodbye, eager to be alone to process my thoughts without a two-year-old trying to climb on me. To add to that, my overbearing sister is trying to set me up with a guy who I'm certain is a virgin and has never been on a date before.

When I get into the car, I check my phone, but still no text. Not even a goodbye 'I had to leave to be in someone else's vagina.' Argh, this is what happens when I'm around Ava for more than five minutes.

On the drive home, I crank up the music until I get into the underground parking lot of my apartment. I park in my usual spot, then turn the ignition off, resting my head against the seat for a moment. After a few deep breaths, willing this unknown feeling pressing on my chest to subside, I open the door and gasp.

"Oh my God," I almost shout, clutching at my chest. "What are you doing here?"

Masen is leaning against his black sports car with sleeves rolled up and his arms crossed beneath his chest.

"You didn't answer my question."

I tilt my head in confusion. "Maybe I didn't get the chance because you left again like the Phantom of the Opera. Is this your thing now? Up and leave without a goodbye?"

He drops his gaze to the garage floor, then raises his eyes at a slow pace until they meet with mine.

"Addison," he grits.

I move closer to him, fueled by anger like his behavior is acceptable.

"What? Say whatever it is you need to say. I'm a big girl and can handle the truth."

His hand reaches out for the top of my sweatpants, pulling me into him as our lips crash together. I let out a moan, pressing my hands on his chest while our tongues battle feverishly. The heat of his skin against my stomach ignites desperation within me to have his touch all over me.

We both pull away at the same time, out of breath. Slowly, Masen traces his finger up my chest until he reaches my face. At a slow and agonizing pace, he runs his thumb along my bottom lip.

"I believe we agreed to you returning the favor," he murmurs.

My hands wander on their own accord, resting on the top of his suit pants. With my gaze still fixated on him, I manage to unclasp the top then pull his zipper down.

I'm drawn to his lips, placing my mouth on his to taste him while I slide my hand inside his boxers to wrap around his cock. A strangled moan is trapped between our heated kisses as I gently slide my hand toward the tip but something odd rubs against my skin.

I pull back with ragged breaths, gazing at him with curiosity.

"I guess my instincts were right. You've never been with a man who's pierced."

All my senses are hyperaware, the curiosity killing me. I tug his boxers and pants down without a word, then slowly slide down his body, so I'm staring at it with my own eyes.

"Holy shit," I whisper, admiring how perfect his cock stands in front of me with the barbel shining like a golden ticket.

"Like what you see, sweetheart?"

My eyes raise to meet his. "I'll ask you the same question." My lips part as I stick my tongue out and run it along the tip of his piercing. "Like what you see?"

He wraps his hands around my head, not allowing me another moment to tease him. My mouth opens wide, taking him in as much as I can. I move at a fast pace, desperate to relieve the throb between my legs. The faster I move, the harder he grunts, but I'm unable to control my own need to come.

I pull back momentarily, but he refuses for me to stop. "I know you're soaking wet, Miss Edwards. I expect your sweet little pussy to come for me just like I came for you last night."

And with that said, I don't hold back any longer.

My tongue plays with his piercing, gaining momentum as his grip around me tightens. I'm addicted to the taste of him, the power I hold at this moment as he begs me to open my mouth wide so he can come in my mouth.

Then, his muscles tighten, and his groan is fierce as he blows inside my mouth. At the same time, I explode in my underwear.

"Fuck," I moan, closing my eyes while swallowing all of him.

My knees are weak, willing to collapse, but I manage to stand up, so we're face to face. Quickly, he pulls his pants and boxers back up before anyone actually catches us.

I try to catch my breath, unsure what to say now it's over.

"So, we're even," I tell him with a slight choke on my words.

"Yes, we are."

Just as I'm about to say thanks for a good time, it was great, and I guess I'll see you around sometime, my phone begins to ring. Cruz's number flashes on the screen.

"Are you okay?" I answer, knowing he's been out drinking.

"Addy, you know I love you, right?"

"Cruz, what's wrong? Where are you?"

He laughs through the phone. "Still here. I just wanted to call to say I love you."

"Great, I love you too. Now, how are you getting home?"

"U... Uber," he stumbles out.

"Okay," I say, taking a deep breath. "I'm coming to pick you up. The fact that you can't even say the word 'Uber' means you probably can't book one either. I'll be there in twenty minutes."

I hang up the call as Masen glances at me while grimacing.

"Why are you looking at me that way?"

"My brother is old enough to take care of himself."

My head flinches back as I try to understand his sudden mood change.

"He is, but he's also my best friend. I don't necessarily agree with him getting drunk, but it's his life. He's young, and I'd rather know he gets home safely than wandering the streets where God knows what will happen."

Masen nods, adopting a sullen look. He runs his fingers through his dark brown hair, unable to look my way.

"We said this was it," I remind him, turning away as well. "I should go get him."

I expect him to say something about Cruz, but instead, he walks to the other side of the car and opens the driver's door.

"I'll see you around," he simply says, void of any emotion.

A small pang stabs my chest. What did I expect? An amicable parting from a man who disappears every time we disagree over something.

I've learned my lesson. Masen Cooper is all about himself.

And I'm done playing this game.

Ready to get out before I become the victim.

TEN

MASEN

"Masen, I expect you to be on your best behavior tonight."

Mom is standing inside my bedroom with four different tuxedos, all of which look the same. She hangs them up for me to choose one, so I point to the far left to get her off my back.

I'm sitting up in bed, dressed in my sweats and white tee with my laptop beside me. When she called me early this morning, I didn't expect her to turn up an hour later for a last-minute fitting. The last thing I want is to mingle with people I don't care for. It's the pitfall of the corporate world, smile but keep a watch on your rivals.

"When have I ever caused trouble?" I question her.

Mom stills her movements, placing her hand on her hip. "How about the award ceremony in Vegas?"

The corner of my lips quirks up at the memory. "I think you can blame your husband for that. He started the shots at the bar."

A small huff escapes Mom. "You're right. Your father is always the instigator of trouble at these events. Given Lex and Noah will be there, I guess tonight will end up no different. Oh, and Adriana is coming but no Julian because he's in Haiti interviewing for a documentary."

Dad is notorious for ordering shots when there's an event he deems boring. I don't mind. His antics leave everyone in laughing fits. All but Mom, she usually leaves him to find his own way home then gets him back when he's battling the hangover from hell.

"Oh, and before I forget, your brother will be joining us."

"Great," I mutter with boredom.

"He's bringing a date. Maybe you should too?"

This time, I let my annoyance be heard. "C'mon, Mom, why do these events always require a date?"

Mom ignores my question, running her hand along the tux to make sure there are no creases. I assume the conversation is over so I focus my attention back on my emails. As I begin to type a heated message back to a supplier who has been dodging our calls, Mom turns around and glances at me with a serious expression.

"Masen, I've never once asked you to change your lifestyle. You remind me a lot of your father, and I recognize you're young and still sowing those wild oats of yours."

If only she knew.

"But... I'm waiting," I grumble.

"It doesn't hurt to show others you're capable of being more than a man who sleeps around for his own pleasure."

With a flat look, my eyes narrow at her unjust treatment. I'm failing to understand why I should care about what others think of me. It goes against everything she taught me.

"I'm not getting into this argument again with you," I warn her, trying to suppress my anger.

She raises her hands in the air. "Fine, if your brother can take Addison, I don't see why it's so difficult for you to bring someone as well."

My fingers stop typing as the blood rushes through me like water bursting sandbanks during a torrential storm. *So, all along her date is my brother?*

A million different things are running through my head. Is something actually going on between them? I heard the phone call, him professing how much he loves her. Best friends don't do that. I'm close to Ava, and half the time, she calls me a dick, never ever telling me how much she loves me. And it goes the same way for me. Love is a strong fucking word to use, and it sounded very much to me that something is going on.

But none of it makes sense. If there was, in fact, something between them, why was she sucking me off in the parking lot like I was her last meal on Earth?

I must find out for myself.

And if my brother is bringing a date to this event, then it's only fair that I do too.

A rasp leaves my throat as I clear it, trying to remain calm. "You're right, Mom. I'll bring someone suitable. After all, eyes are on me to be the next CEO."

Mom walks over, placing her hand on my cheek. "You already are CEO, honey. Perhaps your father needs to make that clear."

Wearing tuxedos for work events is a ridiculous notion.

Yet I play the part, with my date's arm linked in mine as we walk in. Ariel is her name, a former Miss USA contestant who isn't so bad in bed. Sure, she squeals more than I enjoy, but it was one-time last year and not exactly worthy of going back for seconds.

Tonight, though, I need her for an entirely different reason.

The ballroom is located in West Hollywood and is one of the newer spaces in the area. The layout is simple but decorated in black and gold, which is the color of our branding. Our marketing team is on point with everything tonight, and Mom made sure only the best media outlets were in attendance.

As for Dad, he's circulating the room with his pretend face to impress everyone.

"C'mon, let's have a drink."

I grab Ariel's hand though her silver gown is long and beaded, making it difficult for her to move fast. The bartender serves us straight away, so I order Ariel champagne while I go for something more to my liking—bourbon.

"Well, Mr. Cooper, it's been a while."

Beside me, Lex is standing with Charlie at his side. His emerald eyes are probing me like he knows what I've done with his daughter. I bury the paranoia to extend my hand and shake his own.

"Yes, it has been, Lex. How are you?"

"Good," he says, then turns to face Charlie. "Great, if I'm being honest."

Charlie leans over and kisses me hello. For someone Mom's age, the woman is sexy. If she weren't married to a tycoon who's also my dad's best friend, I'd be trying to get her on all fours and beg her to scream my name.

Fuck, what the hell is wrong with you?

Lex would kill me with his bare hands for even thinking it.

Dad appears with a drink in hand, looking bored as he walks over here. It's not long before Adriana arrives and joins us. According to Mom, Kate was called to a family emergency in England this afternoon, and Noah decided to fly over with her for support.

"What time am I officially allowed to order shots?" Dad

asks with a forced grin. "If I have to speak to Jonathan McIntyre about his beloved horses again, I'm seriously going to strangle the man."

Adriana laughs. "You mean Desmond and Gloria?"

"Who the hell names their horses Desmond and Gloria?" Dad shakes his head but eagerly drinks his whisky, then slams the glass on the bar demanding another.

"Someone..." Lex adds, then continues, "... who has more money than he knows what to do with."

Dad cocks his head as he glances at Lex. "How come you're not part of his horse club, then?"

"Because I still have a beautiful wife who deserves my attention," Lex responds with a knowing smile.

"How romantic of you," Charlie gushes, placing her hand on her heart. "Now, was that before or after the strip club visit last Saturday?"

"Firstly, it wasn't a strip club," Lex corrects her.

"It's true, Charlie," Adriana claims, raising her glass for no apparent reason. "It was a client's bar, and someone forgot to mention the dress code for the event."

"Topless waitresses are not a dress code," Charlie argues back.

Dad laughs. "Look, it was Noah's invite. We just tagged along."

Charlie throws her arms up in the air. "Of course, blame my cousin since he isn't here."

"I'm pretty certain this has Eric's name all over it," the voice behind me says.

The sound of her voice sends this frenzy within me. I'm careful not to turn around too quickly, not wanting to appear too eager to those around me, especially her parents.

But slowly, I do so until I'm staring into her emerald eyes. Fuck, why can't I breathe?

"Addison, honey. You're here." Charlie hugs her daughter, followed by Lex. "And who's your handsome date?"

Cruz leans in for a hug. "The guy who begged his best friend."

My brother then turns to face me, giving me a simple nod. I don't say anything, still fixated on how stunning she looks in a red off-the-shoulder gown. Her hair is out, styled to the side, exposing her delicate skin.

"Addison, twice in one week. Isn't that something," I muse.

"Rather coincidental..." she trails off, glancing at Ariel beside me. "Will you introduce your girlfriend to us?"

"Ariel..." I begin with, leaning over to gesture, "... is a friend and here to accompany me tonight."

Dad snickers, shaking his head while finishing his second drink. "Your mother got to you."

I casually introduce Ariel to everyone before she excuses herself to use the restroom. The moment she's gone, Cruz slaps my arm proudly. "Damn, bro. Not bad at all."

Lex hides his grin behind his drink as Charlie glances at him with a death stare.

"I'm not sure why you're looking at me like that," he tells her.

"You encourage bad behavior."

Dad lets out a long whistle. "Son, there are moments when I wonder if my guidance is any use to you. But once again, I'm proven my influence is well-appointed. Good job."

"Good job?" Addison blurts out of nowhere, only to realize she's done so. "Ariel looks like she's an intelligent woman, not some bimbo who's placed on some sexist pedestal for male gratification."

"Addy," Cruz chuckles. "It's a joke."

"I'm going to get a drink," she tells him.

"The bar is right here."

"Well, I'm going to the other side of the bar. Excuse me, everyone."

Addison walks away, unable to look my way. I can't exactly chase after her, so I stand here, hoping everyone leaves so I can ask her what the hell that was about. Talk about causing an unnecessary scene.

"I don't know what's up with her. She's been anxious all week," Cruz confesses.

"Addison, anxious?" Adriana and Charlie say at the same time.

Cruz shrugs his shoulders. "Yeah, maybe it's the new job, I dunno."

"I'm going to go make sure she's okay," Charlie informs us.

Charlie's motherly worries overtake my chance to speak to her, so instead, I stand around with the rest of them, ordering another drink. As soon as the bartender slides it over, I drink in one go and am about to order another when Dad stops me.

"Save it, kid, let's make it interesting."

Dad orders tequila for everyone, surprising us all since it's early into the night, and usually, his shot ordering is toward the end when all the essential people leave.

When the bartender finishes serving, Mom joins us with a disappointed look on her face. "Really, Haden, this early?"

"Yes, this early. You can thank me later."

Mom bows her head, hiding her grin only for me to catch the hidden meaning behind that comment and her grin. Jesus fucking Christ. Why are my parents so twisted? It's the perfect reason to excuse myself. I'm not staying around for Dad's dirty talk.

I see Charlie walk back through the crowd, leaving Addison behind at the bar. I make my way over, stopping during the short walk to greet people, then slide up beside her.

"What's with the outburst back there?"

"It was nothing," she's quick to respond. "I just didn't know you'd be here."

"And is me being here with Ariel a problem for you?"

Addison's eyes dart to mine. "No, why would it be?"

My head flinches back, slightly confused as to her sudden mood swings.

"Well, you're here with a date."

"Yeah, your brother."

"Right, it's always about Cruz."

"What's that supposed to mean?" she argues back.

My name is called, prompting us both to turn around. Ariel appears with a smile on her face when she sees me, linking her arm back into mine. Addison's gaze falls to where Ariel touches me softly, but then she quickly turns away.

"Your mom asked me to find you. There are a few speeches needed. Then apparently, the night is ours."

I turn to say something but keep my mouth shut and walk away.

The speeches were organized to be held earlier in the night, so the old folk attending didn't have to hang around. Dad says a few words, his public speaking A-game on as usual. I follow him and talk about our future projects, to which the crowd applauds us.

Instead of formal dining, servers walk around with hors d'oeuvres and appetizers on platters. I grab a few things, but tonight, my appetite is less than par. The liquor is more appetizing and calms whatever the hell is going on inside me.

People begin to fill the dance floor, and it's not long before my brother drags a hesitant Addison to do the same. He grabs her hand, a simple move causing my chest to burn with annoyance, then when they're amongst the others dancing, he wraps his hands around her waist and pulls her into him.

I throw back the bourbon in hand, losing count of how many I've had. Every time I see her laugh in his arms, the jealousy spreads through me like an ugly disease, willing my heart to stop beating at any moment.

Then, my instincts kick in. If Addison wants to have her fun, then I'll have mine.

My hand drops to Ariel's, pulling her to the dance floor. Ariel is pleased, wrapping her arms around my neck while I rest my hands on her hips. She smells nice but *not* nice enough.

"How long do we have to stay here tonight?"

My eyes dart to Addison, the same time, she braves my gaze. She presses her lips flat, adopting a pinched expression.

"Masen?"

I shake my head. "Sorry, what did you ask?"

Ariel leans in to whisper, "What time can we leave, so I can suck that beautiful cock of yours?"

Her dirty words aren't lost on me, but my attention is back onto Addison, who lets go of Cruz and walks toward the exit, leaving him alone on the dance floor.

"Excuse me, I need to take care of something."

My hands fall from Ariel's hips as I glance around to make sure no one notices where I'm going. Addison exits the ballroom, turning left toward the restroom. I pick up my speed until I'm at arm's length. My grip tightens around her arm, forcing her to turn around in shock. There's a set of double doors leading into an empty ballroom beside us. I quickly drag her inside the empty room, which is darker than the main area, with only the lights shining from beneath the closed door and dimly lit lighting near the exit sign.

"Are you crazy?" she grits, pulling her arm from my grip. "What if someone saw us?"

I pace the area between us, running my hands through my hair, willing myself to calm the hell down.

"What the hell was that back there? All night you've had some chip on your shoulder and acting like a goddamn bitch."

"What do you want from me?" Her eyes are wild, just like mine. "You bring some woman who no doubt you'll fuck tonight, and I'm supposed to say what to you?"

"And you think you're all innocent in this?"

The fire is burning in her eyes, her nostrils flaring as she stares with such contempt.

"I'm walking away before I say something I'll regret later."

I grab her arm again, turning her around before I push her against the wall. Our lips are only inches apart, and the need to have her is driving me insane.

"I'm not done with you." I breathe.

"You're dangerous," she whispers, unable to look at me. "Once the line is crossed..."

"You'll never want another man inside you again."

My mouth crashes onto hers, desperate to taste her sweet tongue battle against mine. I lose all sense of control with her, kissing every part of her exposed neck until my hands reach around and tug her zipper down. I don't stop to think of being caught, needing her tits exposed so I can devour them like the hungry and selfish beast I am when around her.

The moment the top of her dress falls, her chest is fully bare, causing me to lick my lips in delight.

"So, fucking, beautiful."

Even in the dim light, her nipples are a perfect shade of pink, calling my name as I take them in my mouth. I tug on them with my teeth, hearing her moan as her hands wrap around my head while pleading with me to tug harder.

My cock is throbbing with every moan escaping her beautiful lips. I know she wants me, desperate to have me enter her.

But I'm not going to play nice, not after she teased me on the dance floor with my own flesh and blood.

I play dirty to get what I want.

And I want her.

My hand moves beneath her dress, scrambling to get inside her panties and finger her tight pussy. I thrust my fingers into her, groaning as they slide so effortlessly. Careless in my actions, I keep finger-fucking her roughly, relishing in how soaked her pussy becomes and the sound it makes, which is driving me to the brink of insanity.

Inside my pants, I'm ready to fucking blow. All this control I had, perhaps I'm fucking wrong. I'm tormenting myself just as much.

I need her to beg for it.

"You want me to fuck you?" I ask, grazing her clit with my finger.

She raises her hands to grab my face, pressing her lips against mine for a deep kiss before briefly pulling away.

"I think you need to fuck me," she challenges confidently. "Get me out of your system since I'm the only Edwards girl willing to fuck you."

I cock my head. "Is that so?"

Addison runs her finger down my chest. "You've tasted me, and I've tasted you. So, this is it. You fuck me, and then we walk away, no strings attached. We're not friends, so we can't be friends with benefits."

"So, you're telling me this is a hate fuck?"

She nods, moving her hands to my pants and unbuttoning the top. "It sure is. Now fuck me like you know you hate me."

I quickly unzip my pants, releasing my cock. I stroke it slowly as I watch her, savoring every moment. Her eyes hungrily watch my cock as I increase my strokes, spreading the pre-cum all over my hands.

My chest is pounding and pulling her roughly toward me, my lips crash against hers. The wait is killing me, my patience growing thin by the sheer desire running through my veins.

"Are you ready for me?"

"Wait," she murmurs. "We need protection."

Fuck, how could I forget? I pull my wallet to retrieve a condom. There's one inside, but God knows how long I've had it since I usually have sex at home and not in public. Tearing the corner, I quickly place it on, desperate to be inside her.

This stall of action is killing me, so I spread her legs to lift her, pressing her against the wall for support. She wraps her legs around my waist as I ease her on my cock.

She's so fucking tight, just the way I've always imagined.

The ache causes me to groan. Shutting my eyes tight, I hold back from finishing too early. Taking small breaths, I manage to stop the climactic finish and slam my body against hers. She begs for me to fuck her harder, moaning as my cock goes in deeper.

"Why do you have to be such a jerk?" she questions with a moan following. "If you weren't, you could've fucked me as much as you wanted to."

I slow down my movements. "Dangerous words coming from you, Miss Edwards. I warned you, once you've had me inside you, you'll never want anyone else."

Her head rests against the wall, eyes closed as moans continue to leave her lips.

"Your piercing... it's..." She's unable to string together a sentence.

I lean in with my cock still inside her. Pushing her hair aside, my teeth graze her ear. I remain still for a moment, listening to her heartbeat, admiring the glow of sweat lingering on her skin. Her breathing slows, but I know she's anxious. Her tight pussy is wrapped around my cock, and I know she's almost there, holding back just like me, wanting this to last as long as possible.

"We can't stay here all night. Someone will see me fucking your sweet pussy. So, I have no choice but to make you come," I warn her.

"Then I better not stop you, Mr. Cooper."

She scrapes her thumb on my bottom lip, causing the feverish spell within me to intensify.

"Come with me," I demand with a rasp. "I want you to come with me."

The palms of my hands grip onto her ass cheeks tightly, our foreheads touching as I thrust inside her. She rides my cock, a rhythm building momentum until all I feel is her muscles tighten around my shaft. My body jerks forward, a shiver following as a deep grunt escapes me, and my body basks in euphoria.

My eyes blink rapidly, sweat dripping off my forehead while I try to gather my bearings and gain visibility again. The momentary flash of lights blinds me as does the pleasure overcoming every inch of my body. My skin is on fire beneath my formal white shirt and tuxedo jacket.

Our breaths, uneven, echo inside the room.

Slowly, she slides herself off, leaving me with one full condom. I slide it off, searching around to find a trash can in the corner. Quickly, I button my pants and discard the condom, hoping it's buried enough inside the trash bag for cleaners not to notice.

As I walk back, Addison is fixing her dress but unable to zip the back.

"Here, let me help you."

She turns around, allowing me full access to her open

back. Her skin is glowing, and I want nothing more than to strip her entirely bare and kiss every single inch of her.

My fingers tug on the zipper, pulling it back up until it's in place.

"Addison..."

"You don't need to say anything," she interrupts me, turning back around to look me directly in the eyes. "We were both curious. It's done. We move on, and no one gets hurt."

I ignore the nagging voice inside my head, the one telling me this is too good to be true. A gorgeous woman tells me this was a one-time with no strings attached. Fuck, most men would be laughing to themselves for getting so lucky.

So why is there no laughter? This burning sensation crippling my chest is the only thing I feel right now.

"If that's what you want," is all I say.

Addison's eyes widen, but then she drops her gaze to the floor.

"That's exactly what I want from you."

ELEVEN
ADDISON

My head leans on the passenger window as Cruz rambles incessantly.

"I'm surprised I made it to the end of the night. Corporate people are so stiff and formal," he complains.

Lights move by fast. At the same time, my head spins. I'd lost count of just how much I drank throughout the night, and after I walked out of the empty ballroom, I drank even more just to get through the night.

Masen stayed at the opposite end of the room, keeping his distance and barely looking my way. His date, Ariel, hovered beside him at all times until he made his usual phantom move and disappeared without a goodbye.

It only angered me further, so I drank and drank, allowing Haden to serve me shots. When Dad pulled one off me, I knew I had to stop. His judgment is enough to make anyone stop.

Now, I'm paying the price, and Cruz's erratic driving is causing my stomach to flip into a nauseous wave.

"Addy, you look—"

"Don't say it, okay?"

"Drunk," he blurts out, unapologetic. "What was with you tonight?"

I stare out the window again. "I don't know."

Cruz pulls into the garage at the same time I cover my mouth, then swiftly open the door in time to throw up all over the floor.

"Jesus Christ, Addy. I don't think I've ever seen you this wasted."

My head continues to spin, forcing Cruz to carry me all the way to the apartment. When we get inside, he suggests I shower, but I'm too tired, desperate for bed.

As soon as I hit the pillow, my eyes fall shut.

I turn my body onto my side, moaning through the aches ripping through my entire body. The room is bright, indicating it's daylight. Somehow, I manage to stumble to the kitchen in hopes of finding some Advil and a fresh brew of coffee.

"Good morning, sunshine."

'You're too loud," I grumble.

"Okay, sorry," he says in a quieter tone. "What do you want? Breakfast? Advil? Coffee?"

My arms are sitting on the table, so I rest my head on them and close my eyes. "All of the above."

"Coming right up."

Cruz does his best-friend duty, turning on the coffee machine and whipping up some breakfast. I manage to drink, eat, and stay awake for the entire duration. After I'm done, I head back to bed again, only to wake up around midday.

This time, I feel much better. With nothing else to do, I take a quick shower then settle on the couch and stream some shows. Cruz snuggles beside me, arguing over my choices since he wants action or at least a thriller.

On the coffee table, my phone is pinging like crazy. Of course, the group chat.

> **AVA**
> Is there something you want to tell us, Addy?

The muscles inside my chest begin to tighten as panic sets in. Surely, Masen wouldn't have told her anything? He wouldn't dare.

> **ME**
> Like what?

> **JESSA**
> Oh... spill, Ava.

> **LUNA**
> Addy got blind drunk last night drinking shots with Haden and Uncle Lex had to stop her.

> **MILLIE**
> Wait, with Haden? I smell age gap affair.

> **AVA**
> Hey, let's not disrespect Presley.

> **LUNA**
> I'd so do Haden, especially with the piercing.

> **AVA**
> How do you know about the piercing?

> **LUNA**
> Your mom? I dunno... I think Jessa told me.

> **JESSA**
> Hey! You weren't supposed to tell anyone.
> Kate told me not to say anything.

> **AVA**
> Ladies, back to Addy, please.

> **ME**
> So I drank a bit more than usual. So what?
> And to clarify, many of us drank with Haden.
> Not just me.

AVA

According to Masen, you were on some roll last night Miss Attitude.

I sit up, pushing Cruz away complaining he just found his groove. I re-read the message, trying to read between the lines. So, Ava spoke to Masen. But what did he say?

ME

Is that what he said?

AVA

Yeah, that's it. I texted him when he was dropping his date home. It caught me by surprise he wasn't in bed with her. Must have been a full moon last night, everyone was acting weird. Remember the pool boy I had a crush on who the parentals hired? I ran into his mother at the hospital. Turns out he was a she pre-pool boy career.

MILLIE

Ava, are you even surprised?

The group chat continues to which Ava goes on about the lengths she'd go to seduce Henrik, our pool boy. I silence my notifications, sitting back quietly to attempt to watch the movie.

But all I can think about is last night and how he *didn't* jump into bed with her.

Eric is sitting across from me after dropping by the office to see if I was available for lunch. I welcomed the invitation, eager to pick his brain before I officially go insane.

"I'd like to ask you a hypothetical question for research purposes."

Eric nods with an eager smile. "Is it about how Adriana can squirt multiple times if she's being fingered?"

I choke on my saliva, coughing out loud as people around the café watch on. The attention is embarrassing, to say the least.

"Oh my God," I whisper, leaning in. "No, and what the hell are you talking about? I can't even with you and your brain sometimes."

"It's just baffling, that's all," he says nonchalantly.

"I think I just lost my appetite. You do know she's my aunty, right?"

"Yes, but aren't you the least bit curious?"

"No," I tell him firmly. "And don't you dare bring up Mom. I'm well aware my parents still have sex. It doesn't mean you need to go into detail."

"Fine, then what's your question?"

My fingers trace the edge of the plate, coordinating my thoughts before I speak. The worse thing I can do right now is accidentally blurt out I fucked Masen inside the ballroom as my parents danced on in the next room.

"One-night stands..."

Eric gasps, clutching his hand to his chest before he places it on mine with wide eyes.

"I'm ready. Ask me all the questions."

"So..." I drag, followed by a hard swallow. "Is it called a one-night stand if, in fact, there have been three instances?"

"Honey bear, I need proper details," Eric informs me with a serious face.

"Okay, so say the first time, the guy kinda, um, went down on the woman..."

"Eating the panty hamster, gotcha."

I glance sideward, unsure how to take the term 'panty hamster' seriously, but it's Eric, so I find a way to continue.

"And then the second time, she goes down on him."

"Slurpin' the gherkin, totally hot." He nods with pursed lips while fanning himself. "And the third time?"

"The actual deal."

Eric lets out a long whistle. "Girl, this is complicated."

"I figured," I mutter beneath my breath.

"Okay, well, let's look at this logically. Going down on someone is hot, but we all know it leaves you with too much curiosity. Sex is sex. Just because a guy can eat pussy doesn't mean he knows how to fuck like a wild stallion."

My eyes widen in panic. "Will you keep your voice down?"

"So, to answer your question, I'd called this situation a fling. Not a one-night stand."

I lean back into the chair, picking at my bread. "Good to know."

Eric lifts his glass, taking a sip of his iced tea quietly before placing it down. He carefully picks a small piece of fluff off his canary yellow shirt then focuses his attention back on me.

"So, how long do I sit here before you tell me who it is?"

"It's no one, a hypothetical."

Eric crosses his arms beneath his chest. "Don't lie to me, Addison Kate Edwards. You've got a glow on your cheeks. A blow-job glow."

My hands move to my cheeks on their own accord. They feel fine, but I panic anyway and grab my compact out of my purse to check.

"Who's been cleaning your cobwebs, girl?"

"Eric, like I said, hypothetical. As for the red cheeks, talking about such topics makes me uncomfortable. It's something I must improve on if I want a career of listening to people because sex talk will come up."

"You're a terrible liar," Eric deadpans. "I give you one week before you're at my doorstep begging for advice because your fling has sailed into dangerous waters."

I tilt my head in confusion. "Dangerous waters?"

"A relationship."

The afternoon proves busy with appointments scheduled almost back to back. I welcome the distraction, allowing me not to dwell on Eric's parting words.

Dr. Jenner spends an hour with me going through some of her cases. As she talks, I listen attentively, jotting down a few notes of my own. She's an intelligent woman, and I can see why she's paid top dollar for her consults.

Once again, it's late and well past my ordinary hours. The only downfall to being part-time is the paperwork piles up on my days off. My phone beeps beside me when the final notes are entered into the system.

> MASEN
>
> Just to make it clear, I didn't go home with Ariel.

I type quickly, surprised he even bothered to text me this information since it's clear he got what he wanted.

> ME
>
> Did you drop her off at the wharf then wave goodbye when she disappeared into the water like the good little mermaid she is?

> MASEN
>
> Funny. Are you jealous?

> ME
>
> You're single. Therefore, jealousy isn't appropriate in such circumstances.

> MASEN
>
> Talking like a professional. By the way, you never actually picked up the manuscript the other night. You were clearly distracted. I'm assuming you still want it?

ME

Yes, I do still want it.

MASEN

I'm at my office. If you want it, come get it.

I smell the trap, see it from a distance. My phone is still in my hands, but my fingers won't type. If I see him again, can I forget about everything that has happened? Surely, I can. It's out of my system. I straighten my shoulders, grab my purse, and shut down my computer.

Masen's office is within walking distance from my car, so I opt to walk in the fresh air rather than drive. When I enter the building, the temperature increases, and each step to the elevator becomes more challenging.

Calm down, you can do this, plus you need to know what happens at the end of the story.

The elevator door pings open. It's empty, thank God, so I enter before hitting the button to his floor. When I reach level nine, I exit and walk straight to his office without thinking. The door is partially open, but I don't even knock, watching him type an email as I close the door behind me. This time, he's wearing reading glasses, something he hasn't worn in front of me.

Great, now he has to look extra sexy.

He glances up, followed by a cocky sneer playing on his lips.

"Miss Edwards," he says, leaning back into his chair. "Do I have something you want?"

"Yes, we've discussed this. I want to know how the story ends."

Masen slides the manuscript forward. I walk toward the table, reaching out for it, but he grabs my wrist instead.

"That's not all you came for, now, is it?"

I lower my head, unable to look him in the eyes. My body

is betraying me on all accounts, growing hot and feverish with an ache between my legs. The beat of my heart is loud and erratic, I'm certain he can hear the abnormal sound through my chest.

He lets go of my wrist, moving off his chair and around the table. The heat radiates off his body as he closes in behind me.

"Masen... I..."

"What is it, Addison? Tell me what you want?"

His hands rest on my hips, but then I hear his breathing become louder.

"Fuck me," I whisper.

Masen pushes his body against my ass, his hard cock teasing me once again. Then, he leans in and brushes his lips against my ear lobe. "Good girl, if you ask, you shall receive."

And with those words, he doesn't leave a moment to spare, lifting my skirt and pushing my black lace panties aside. He somehow manages to undo his pants as his cock springs free and knocks on my entrance. I moan in agony, desperate for him to enter me, but then he stops.

"I don't have protection on me," he confesses in an agitated tone.

My head falls to which my eyes close.

Fuck it. You only live once.

"Enter me," I beg of him.

He doesn't wait for me to change my mind, sliding in with desire driving him to pump me hard. I keep my voice down, aware someone can hear us at any time.

"Come for me, Addison," he demands.

I reach behind and pull him into me. At the same time, my body falls into a euphoric state. Every inch of me is sensitive to movement and touch, but then I realize he hasn't finished. A few more thrusts, and he pulls out with a grunt.

Catching my breath, I turn around to see him with his chest rising and falling at a manic pace.

But my eyes fall elsewhere, to his hand beside his cock, all covered in his cum.

I reach for his hand as he watches me with curiosity. Bringing it up to my lips, I run my tongue along his skin and lick the cum from his hand.

"Fuck," he groans.

When I'm finished, I hold his stare and fall to my knees, cleaning up the rest of him.

"You're still hard," I murmur, circling my tongue around his piercing.

"Because I'm not finished with you yet."

"Oh..."

"But not here," he says in a strained voice while watching me lick him clean.

"Where?"

"My place. I need every inch of you naked, Addison."

I pull back, unable to hide my grin. "You lead, I'll follow, Mr. Cooper."

Masen quickly buttons his pants, but then, in a sudden move, he cups my face and plants a soft kiss on my lips.

"You sure you can handle it?"

I kiss him back, burying my smile. "We'll soon see."

TWELVE

ADDISON

Masen lives in a penthouse apartment only a few blocks down from the office.

Although the drive only took less than five minutes, several minutes were getting out of the underground parking lot. I'm relieved at the short drive since making small talk after you've fucked a man inside his office is awkward next level.

What can I possibly talk about? The weather or rising gas prices? Thankfully, a call came through on Masen's phone, forcing him to answer it. The client, I assume, stirs Masen's anger as he clenches his teeth while trying to respond calmly. When we arrive at the garage, the call ends too.

"Is everything okay?" I ask to be polite.

"Just incompetency."

I don't say another word, observing him clutch at the steering wheel with white knuckles. The stress is getting to him, or perhaps impatience since his jaw is tight. *Why does he look so hot when he's angry?*

Just as I'm about to give him an out so he can focus on

work, he removes his grip from the wheel and places his hand on my thigh.

"Let's go upstairs."

A small elevator will take us from the parking garage to the penthouse. Masen swipes his key as he enters, but when the doors close, he pins me against the mirror walls and kisses me feverishly.

I'm out of breath when I pull away, wondering how my body is reacting with such desperation when not even an hour ago, he made me come inside his office. Every single touch ignites a new fire, burning hot through my veins.

"I want you completely naked on my bed," he growls into my ear.

His hands slide beneath my skirt, raising it and cupping my ass.

"There are cameras in here," I remind him.

"And?"

I pull away, struggling to still my breathing while adjusting my skirt.

"Surely, you can wait a few minutes?" I tease, gazing into his hazel eyes behind his glasses. "And since when do you wear glasses?"

"Does it bother you?"

My head falls with a knowing grin. "Quite the opposite."

The door pings open to the penthouse floor. Masen takes my hand into his, then enters his pin code. When the door opens, curiosity gets the better of me. My eyes trawl the main living room, noting how minimalistic the furniture is. The color palette is browns and neutrals, but catching my attention is the large dark oak bookshelf occupying the entire wall. It's filled with so many books, which shouldn't come as a surprise since Masen works for a publishing house.

"Wow, so many books." I let go of his hand, moving

toward the shelf to observe the literature he's collected. "I didn't realize you read so much."

"I do, not so much romance unless I'm forced to."

I turn around with a smile. "So, we do have something in common?"

He nods with a smirk. "That we do."

"Do I get a tour of the grand digs?"

"Sure."

He takes my hand again and leads me through the living room and to the kitchen. There's an adjoining dining room with a long table. It seems rather big for someone who probably dines by himself, but I keep my opinion at bay.

"And the bedroom?" I ask at the same time his hand grips tighter. "You always have to save the best for last."

"Is that so?" He rubs his chin until we're standing inside his room. "Is it what you expected?"

Much like the living room, the space is simple. The king-sized bed has a navy-blue headboard with white sheets on top of the mattress. The bed itself doesn't catch my attention, but the large window overlooking the city does.

"This view is amazing," I say in awe. "I have a view of a brick wall which belongs to a questionable massage parlor."

Masen moves behind me, wrapping his hands around my waist as his lips find my neck. His kisses are teasingly gentle, enough to make me close my eyes and give into him.

"You're very distracting," he murmurs, sliding his hand inside my white blouse and into my bra. "What shall I do with you?"

"Hmm, I have an idea."

With ease, I turn around, so we're facing. My fingers move to his gray business shirt to unbutton each button until his chest is completely exposed. His torso is entirely cut-up, leaving me breathless with just how defined his abs are.

Next, I remove his pants and boxers but not before he

kicks off his socks and shoes. As he stands naked in front of me, I swallow at the sight of his hard cock, demanding attention.

I begin to remove my clothing as he watches while stroking his cock. How can such a simple move be so damn hot? My eyes refuse to turn away. Then when I'm completely naked, I get down on my knees, no longer able to resist.

With my mouth open wide, I take him all in, allowing the tip to hit the back of my throat. His groans dominate the room, no longer bounded by someone catching us in the midst of a forbidden moment.

Then, he pulls back and demands we go to his bed. He lays with his back against the headboard. "I want you to ride me."

Slowly, I climb on top, easing myself on. A soft moan escapes me at the sensation of his piercing touching a sensitive spot. Every single inch of my body is tingling in mad delight, forcing me to stop momentarily before I explode on the spot.

"I... I need to slow down," I barely manage to say.

He places his hand behind his head, gazing while biting down on the corner of his bottom lip.

"We have all night. This is far from over."

I begin to rock gently, closing my eyes to feel him entirely inside me. This euphoric state I'm in is nothing like I've ever felt before. What we're doing is an addiction waiting to happen. I'd give everything I own to feel this moment for the rest of my life.

Everything Masen does consumes me. The way he stares with hunger, the grunts he makes when I move faster, and just when I can't hold back, I warn him that I'm just about to come.

"No," he states in a raspy voice. "Not yet."

"I can't hold back," I almost choke, out of breath.

"Look at me, Addison." His anchored gaze is weighted with desire. I slow down enough for the air to cool down my erect nipples. My skin is shimmering in sweat, but I don't care at this moment. "I need you to look me in the eyes while you make yourself come."

I nod, unable to speak from a dry throat.

But then, I realized we didn't protect ourselves.

"Shit," I blurt out. "You're not wearing—"

"I won't come inside you."

I've never been with a guy without using a condom. Even though I'm on the pill to regulate my period, the doctor's warning of a one percent chance of getting pregnant is like a siren ringing in my head.

My back arches while I raise my hips slightly to gain momentum, but then I remember his command. I straighten my body, keeping my eyes stationed on him, yet my sight is drawn to the way his jaw tightens.

And in a heartbeat, the familiar build inside my stomach begins to swirl. My skin crawls with goosebumps as the delightful rush spreads all over me. I let out a loud moan, riding him fast as the high continues, holding me captive.

"I need to pull out," he warns me in a hurry.

I don't know what comes over me, but I refuse to stop this feeling, so I push down and grind against him faster until he yanks my hips and throws his head back while expelling a grunt.

Our heavy pants are loud and echo inside the room. It takes several moments to calm down at the same time. My limbs become numb as I slide off his body, collapsing on the bed beside him, only to stare at the ceiling.

Suddenly, I feel vulnerable, so I reach for the pillow behind me to cover my naked body.

"Come here," Masen calls, tugging the sheet so we can climb in.

As I lay on my side, he runs his finger down my cheek.

"I thought we agreed to me pulling out?"

"I'm on the pill."

"I see."

"I'm sorry, I got caught up in the moment. It won't happen again."

He leans in and kisses my lips with ease. My body reacts almost instantly, the first sign—my nipples hardening. *Sweet mother of all things pure, there's no possible way I can go again.*

"I want it to happen again," he confesses. "In fact, I want it to happen again right now."

Against my thigh, he presses his hard cock. How is it possible this man can go three times in one day? Before I even have a chance to say something, he runs his tongue along my earlobe.

"I'm hungry," he prompts with a devious smile gracing his lips. "And you have something I want to eat..."

In the middle of the night, my eyes spring open. The room is dark, with only the city lights illuminating the space. Even the moon is obscured behind the clouds, giving us privacy during our endless fucking. Sometime after the third round, I fell asleep.

My eyes are open, but I'm unable to move my limbs. The tips of my fingers reach to the nightstand to grab my phone and check the time—it's just after midnight.

Several texts from Cruz are on my screen, accompanied by five missed calls.

CRUZ

Addy, where are you?

Jesus woman, pick up your phone.

I'm about to call your dad, like seriously.

I sit up in a panic to check the time of the text. It was sent ten minutes ago. Quickly, I type back.

ME

Sorry, out with some friends and the bar is loud. Didn't hear my phone. I'll be home soon.

The bubble appears, and I wait for a response when Masen stirs beside me.

CRUZ

THANK FUCK. I was worried something had happened to you. Okay, see you soon.

Without realizing it, I release a sigh, placing my phone down. I should probably call an Uber to take me home, knowing the streets aren't safe at night.

"What's wrong?" Masen asks, half-asleep beside me.

"Nothing, Cruz just sent me a text because he was worried I hadn't picked up my phone."

Silence falls between us until he shuffles to sit up beside me.

"Does my brother always check in to see where you are?"

I shrug, pulling the sheet to my chest, aware my back is still exposed.

"I guess so. I don't know. I mean, I'm just used to him always checking in," I confess, then remain quiet to gather my thoughts. "I should go. I told him I'll be home soon."

"It's late and not safe for you to leave."

"I'll call an Uber," I tell him.

"No, you're staying here."

"Masen, I can't just stay here."

"Why not? I'm demanding you stay here for your own safety."

I turn to face him. "And what am I supposed to tell Cruz, huh?"

Masen leans over to grab my phone. He begins typing as my eyes widen in confusion.

"What do you think you're doing?"

He throws the phone in front of me. "Telling your boyfriend you're staying over at a friend's house."

"Cruz isn't my boyfriend," I correct him while grimacing. "He's just worried about me. That's all. I can't believe you sent him a text. You're so infuriating!"

The phone lights up, and sitting on the screen is a text from Cruz.

CRUZ

Ok, see you tomorrow. Love u.

I briefly turn away, knowing Masen will voice his opinion any minute now.

"Aren't you going to respond? I love you too," he mocks.

My gaze flicks back to him as my jaw clenches from the anger brewing inside me.

"You're a jerk. You know that?" I charge with frustration. "What makes you think I want to even stay here with you?"

He reaches out and tugs the bedsheet down. Then, he grabs my wrist and pins me beneath him. My mind is telling me to yell at him to get off me.

But my body is committing the ultimate betrayal.

It wants *more*.

Masen raises my wrists above my head, holding me down as his free hand wanders between my thighs.

I gasp at his touch, the sheer pleasure from his fingers grazing against my clit. I'm held captive to him once again, with no chance of escaping this spell he's put me under.

"If you weren't soaking wet again, I might think you don't want to be here."

"Make me come again," I beg of him.

"Say it louder," he demands, thrusting his fingers inside me so carelessly. "Come on, Miss Edwards. I'm waiting."

I arch my back, bringing my breasts closer to him. He sucks on my nipples, causing my body to melt entirely.

"Please, make me come, now."

A dirty smile plays on his lips. "Good girl. Your wish is my command."

THIRTEEN

ADDISON

There's something to be said about the walk of shame. It gives you too much time to think about all the things you *shouldn't* have done.

Take, for example, fucking someone you loath. Not only once but more times than you can count on your fingers. And as if I need another reminder, the sting between my legs is a pleasant memory of just how large he is and just how rough he took me.

On top, from behind, cowgirl, reverse cowgirl—too many positions to even list.

Was I complaining at the time? Of course not, quite the opposite—I begged for more. I was a woman possessed and succumbed to fantasies I didn't even know existed.

All of it was new to me. The few men I'd been with were not adventurous nor confident in the bedroom, so maybe my sisters were right. I don't know what I'm missing if I've never experienced something. I've tasted the forbidden fruit, and boy is it sweet and sinful.

I leave Masen's apartment with a quick goodbye and no parting words. What is there left to say? We agreed to nothing more, and somehow, we've ended up here. It's not appropriate to call it friends-with-benefits when we aren't friends.

So, maybe Masen is right. It's nothing but a hate fuck.

But how many times can a hate fuck occur before it becomes something else? This is an Eric question, but also, involving Eric can be catastrophic. The last thing I need is to make a big deal out of something which is technically still in the molehill stage. There are no mountains just yet, but if I'm not careful, they're just around the corner, and the climb will be disastrous.

When I arrive at my apartment, Cruz is lying on the couch playing his game. He stops when he sees me, then sits up, eyeing me from head to toe.

"Some girls night you must have had. No offense, but you look like shit."

"Thanks," I mumble, praying my skin doesn't turn red, and he figures out my lie. "I'm going to take a quick shower, then head into work."

I move quickly to avoid any further questions from Cruz. Lying to him onsets guilt, but I can't tell him the truth either. Destroying their family unit isn't something I'm prepared to do, even if Cruz doesn't look fondly at his older brother.

After a quick shower, I change into a fresh outfit for work. Unfortunately, there's no time for coffee, so I choose to get into the office earlier and just grab one there. After the night I had, I suspect it's a double shot kind of day, maybe even triple with how exhausted I am.

The day drags on, or perhaps it's not the day but the weight of my guilt from last night. My head bounces from one thought to another. Guilty one moment, exhilarated the next. I hate him, yet I need him inside me. The mixed emotions do nothing but plague me.

The same goes for my empty inbox since Masen doesn't

bother to text. A simple 'did you get home okay' would suffice.

But it doesn't come.

Not today.

Not the day after.

And not even a week later.

I resign myself to the fact that we indeed had a fling. Now, he's flown the coop and busy removing his clothes for some other clueless woman who succumbs to his sexy ways. Eric was right, even though it pains me to admit it.

It's not like I want anything from Masen, and I'll be damned if I cave and send him a text. What will I even say? Nothing, absolutely nothing. I'm not that girl, clingy and all desperate because he hasn't called or texted.

So, I resort to the next best thing—Ava.

"I'm so glad you have time for lunches now you're not studying full-time," Ava mentions while digging into her pasta Bolognese. "Don't get me wrong, I love being an entrepreneur with the freedom to do what I want, but sometimes it can get lonely during the days. Mom and Millie work, Alexa is still in school, Jessa's in Manhattan now, and Luna is always busy, but I'm not sure why. Don't you think that's odd?"

I wait for my cue to talk since Ava is non-stop today. "Luna is a woman of mystery, that I will agree on."

"I bet she's sleeping with some old sugar daddy, and she doesn't want to admit it."

"Luna's not motivated by wealth, quite the opposite with her."

"Then I'd hate to say it..." Ava trails off, leaning against her chair, "... some daddy then."

My body shudders at the mention of *Daddy*.

"You've got playdates with Millie," I remind her, eager to get off the topic of Luna.

"Yeah, I know." Ava sighs, but then the corners of her mouth curve into a smile. "I'm just glad to hang out with you."

It takes a moment to register as my thoughts are so misplaced with everything going on. When I realize she's said something nice, I quickly smile.

"So, what else is happening in your life?" I ask, trying to map out how to land on the topic of Masen without seeming obvious. "All the men in your life playing nice?"

Ava places her fork down to laugh. "Austin always plays nice. A little overprotective with the new baby here, but I'm enjoying the attention."

"He's an amazing husband."

"I'm a very lucky woman," she responds with her eyes dancing. "Fate did its thing, and look how my life turned out."

With a relaxed smile, I touch her hand. "I'm so happy for both you and Millie."

"Thanks, sis. Now, we just need to find you a man."

"Speaking of men," I begin with, clearing my throat. "Dr. Jenner's nephew is in town, and she's asked me to take him out tonight since he's my age. He's majoring in psych too, so at least we'll have something to talk about."

"Um, excuse me. We've been sitting here for close to an hour, and you only mention this now?"

"Firstly, you were rambling on about stuff. Secondly, this isn't a date."

"But he's single?" Ava questions, cocking her head. "And you're single?"

On a technicality, I'm single. That's if I don't factor my fling, which is now flung, into this.

"Yes, but we agreed to me showing him around. That's not a date by definition."

"Call it what you want. It's a date."

My eyes narrow at my sister. "Can you not go around spreading that?"

"Fine, but is he at least hot?"

"He's not my type," I admit before even thinking.

Yes, of course, because your type suddenly became a pierced man who makes you orgasm multiple times without any effort.

Ava draws back while pressing her lips together. "Addison Edwards has a type? Since when did this happen?"

"I'm just saying, on first impressions based on a photo. He's friend-zoned. He is very handsome, just not my type."

Someone send me a life jacket. My cheeks feel like they're burning with my sister's interrogation.

"Interesting ..."

"It's not interesting at all. Maybe I shouldn't go if I'm giving the wrong impression."

Ava's phone vibrates on the table. She glances over to read the text, then snorts out of nowhere.

"Honestly, men," she complains.

"Austin?"

"No, Masen."

My gaze falls onto the plate in front of me faster than you can say *what the fuck.*

I quickly raise my head with a flat stare. "What's the problem?"

"He's been texting me all week about some business problem, but it's also been a whole week of arguing over sandwiches."

"Sandwiches?"

Ava nods, then roll her eyes. "I know, right? He thinks you have to lay the meat and vegetables in a certain order. But then I argued Subway and their method. It's nonsense, but at least it's entertaining when I push his buttons."

A forced smile remains on my face, yet my brain fails to

understand how Masen has time to argue over the stupidest topic but doesn't send me a single text about last week. Anger begins to seep into my veins, causing my body temperature to rise even though we're sitting outdoors in the fresh air. But then, with a downward gaze, my chest begins to hitch. All signs point to one thing—what happened between us was no big deal, and he's moved on.

Beneath the table, my knees lock together as my shoulders curl over my chest.

"Addy, is everything okay? You look—"

"I'm fine," I talk over her. "Just fine."

Hanging out with Harrison is more fun than I thought it would be.

We laugh a lot and tell anecdotes—the two of us have so much in common. Our conversation is never dull and being around him is refreshing.

"So, let me get this straight? You have a girlfriend back home, but your family doesn't know?"

He nods with a grin. "I'm sleeping with my sister's therapist."

I shake my head, both confused and shocked. "Hold on. I'm assuming she's older?"

"You could say that."

My hand slaps his arm, prompting him to stop as we stand on the promenade.

"She's a qualified therapist? So, I'm guessing late twenties, early thirties?"

"Add another decade or two."

My eyes widen in disbelief. Harrison is an attractive guy. Tall, with an athletic build. His jet-black hair makes his light brown eyes stand out. But this information, wow. Just wow.

"This is all so taboo."

"Yeah," he says with a smirk, "but that's why it's fun."

We take the scenic route home to my apartment while I grill him over his adulterous affair. It's clear he's having fun, and that's the extent of it. Yet it still amazes me how men are programmed differently, able to void themselves of attachment after being intimate with a woman.

Harrison begins to tell me a story about his professor, all the while I nod because my professor does the same things.

I laugh with him. "Thanks for tonight. It's good to be able to just chat to someone about the joys and pitfalls of studying psychology."

"My family and friends just don't understand. Except for my aunt, of course."

"Dr. Jenner is a remarkable woman," I say with pride. "I can't believe she spent five years living in Africa and volunteering at the orphanages. It really puts life in perspective."

"Tell me about it. Unfortunately, I guess, we grow up with privileges and don't have a true understanding of the world until we're faced with reality."

We reach my apartment building. As I glance upward, I notice the lights are on.

"You want to come upstairs? My roommate, Cruz, is home, and he likes to talk about football if you're up for it."

"Sure, I'm one of three boys. If you didn't watch football, you hung out with Mom and her book club or my sister and her Barbies."

I knock into his side playfully. "Don't knock book clubs. They're a healthy expression of opinions in a common environment."

Harrison chuckles. "It started off as women's fiction books, but then a new neighbor joined who just went through a divorce. All of a sudden, the book club is serving cocktails, and they're drunk while talking about men's anatomy."

My hands reach into my purse to grab my keys. I'm unable to find them, distracted by my phone buzzing which I ignore. When I finally find them, I jiggle them in the keyhole and open the door to see Cruz on the sofa sitting beside Masen.

Oh shit.

"Addy," Cruz greets while eyeing Harrison. "Why didn't you pick up your phone?"

I force a smile. "Because I was at dinner with Harrison."

Harrison extends his hand to shake Cruz's. "You must be the roommate."

Cruz returns the gesture, but his expression is less than friendly. "Her best friend as well."

Then, Harrison turns his attention to Masen, doing the same polite thing.

The only thing is, he doesn't know he's shaking hands with the devil. The devil wearing his sexy glasses and a gray suit rendering me speechless.

I quickly pull out my phone and see the last message on the screen.

MASEN

Answer me.

My gaze flicks up when Masen reluctantly shakes his hand without an introduction. His face is anything but inviting, and I've seen this exact expression before. If I didn't know better, I'd think he's jealous. Why? I have no idea.

"Masen's my brother," Cruz mumbles, but his annoyance is evident. "So, why did you guys come back here?"

"Just to show him around, you know..."

It leaves my lips before I even have a chance to think. But, what did it matter? I'm single, with no strings attached to anyone, so my guilt is uncalled for.

I straighten my shoulders, willing my confidence to show.

And across from me, hazel eyes are burning fury-hot beneath the reading glasses. The flame begins to spread, reaching me from where I stand and spreading all over my skin.

This means nothing.

He doesn't own me because I'm not a possession to own.

And the minute a chance presents itself, I'm going to remind him that we're nothing.

The fling has officially been flung.

FOURTEEN

MASEN

All it took was one week before I caved like a goddamn pussy.

The moment she left my apartment the morning after, there was a void. I'd spent all night devouring her body as if she belonged to only me. Then, the moment she left, the air inside the apartment grew stifling hot like it took my ability to breathe with her.

This strange feeling evoked something within me, so I do what I always do when I'm overwhelmed and can't decipher what's going on.

I bury my head in work.

But this time, it wasn't enough to distract me, especially when my parents were sitting inside my office wanting to talk.

"Between you and me..." Mom says as Dad is typing an email on his phone, "...I think your brother has feelings for Addison."

The name catches my attention enough for my gaze to life up a little too quickly.

I clear my throat. "I'm not surprised. They live together now."

The jealousy bleeds through my veins, ready to destroy any chance of coming out of this mess I've created unscathed. My hands clench on the table, but as I raise my eyes, Dad is gazing at me with a sudden focus.

"I honestly never expected him to catch feelings. They've been around each other for their entire life," Mom continues speaking.

Dad furrows his brows, still fixated on me. "Perhaps he senses another lion sleeping in his den."

"You might have a point. Cruz mentioned her going on some date tonight with her boss's nephew. He tried not to sound jealous, but a mother knows her son well."

"A date?" I blurt out.

The second it leaves my mouth, Dad sits back with a smirk on his face. Fuck, the man is intuitive, or maybe I just gave too much away. I straighten my shoulders, switching my mannerisms, so no one mentions anything about my behavior.

"Yes, and so she should date. Addison is a beautiful and smart woman. At the ball the other night, so many men asked me about her. I almost felt terrible for all the attention she got."

"Lex and Charlie sure know how to make beautiful girls," Dad praises while cocking his head at me. "Addison is quite the catch. Beautiful and single. Well, maybe not after tonight if this man knows what's good for him."

What the fuck is that supposed to mean? I do my best to control my anger, desperate to text her and ask the truth. What the fuck would I even say? She's mine, and no one else can go near her?

Perfect.

The devil is sitting on my shoulder, handing me a

bourbon and telling me he'll take care of it. My temper flares and the two people who know me too well are watching me quietly.

"Is everything okay, Masen?" Mom asks, quickly glancing at Dad.

I shake my head then remove my glasses to clean them. "It's just been a tough week. We are growing too big too fast. It's hard enough to find proper real estate for us to operate out of in California, but trying to employ skilled people is a whole other story."

"I'm afraid you're right. Good talent is hard to come by these days. College kids don't want to work in an office starting from the ground up. Social media has swayed them into thinking influencing is the way to go," Mom carries on, equally annoyed by our industry of late. "If we're after older people, they know their worth and dollar value. We just can't afford to hire all top-of-the-tier employees. If we can find a balance with some internships, there's our possible solution to this problem."

"You're right, Presley. Why don't we meet with Lex soon to see what our options are? He's been on the hunt for some commercial property and knows what's on the market within our budget," Dad informs us.

"Sounds like a plan." Mom relaxes her shoulders. "I better start wrapping up since I have dinner with Charlie and Adriana tonight."

Dad raises his brows. "Did I know this?"

"Yes, I told you several times." She shakes her head in annoyance, then forces a smile. "Old age getting to you, Haden?"

"Nice comeback. You'll pay for that later."

I drop my head with a heavy sigh. My parents drive me fucking crazy with their arguing, which turns into sexual banter of some sort.

Mom says goodbye and leaves the two of us alone. I jump straight into some numbers since this is the best opportunity to get Dad to have a look before I start the frustrating task of asking HR to performance manage our accountants. There's one guy I can't stand, wondering why Dad even hired the fucker.

"Now that your mother has left, is there something you'd like to share with me?"

"Not particularly," I drag, keeping a poker face.

"So, nothing to do with a certain Miss Edwards?"

As my upper lip tucks in, my eyes fall toward my hands, which tap the table. But, Mom's voice replays in my head.

Addison is going on a date.

"It's not what you think."

Dad releases a long-winded sigh. "I think you're fucking her and the two of you are in over your heads. Too many things at stake, including your brother."

"Cruz has nothing to do with this."

"That's where you're wrong. Cruz has everything to do with this," Dad cautions, but his tone remains calm. "Take your brother out of the equation, and it's just the two of you doing whatever you please."

"Oh, really? You have met Lex, right?"

"That old fella?" He chuckles. "When Will and Amelia's relationship came out, I'd never seen Lex so angry, and I've known the guy for quite some time."

"Yeah, I remember."

"As for Ava, Lex wasn't angry. Disappointed initially, but you know him. He can't be angry at a grandchild."

"Daddy's favorite girl can never do wrong." I snicker.

"But you," he stalls, then releases a breath. "As long as you don't knock Addison up, you're safe."

"Jesus Christ, Dad. I'm not you, okay?"

Dad chuckles, then crosses his arms beneath his chest. "I got lucky with your mom. Damn lucky."

"Yes, you did. According to her, you were off the rails, and she was the best thing to happen to you."

"No argument from me. But as for you, be careful, Masen. Treat her right. Addison is like a daughter to me. All those Edwards girls are. So don't fuck up whatever it is happening between you."

My feet pace outside Addison's apartment, knowing she isn't here and only my brother is home. Inside my hand, I clutch the manuscript she forgot to take again last week because we were both distracted.

Distracted would be an understatement.

Fucking her sweet-tasting pussy is more accurate.

But now isn't the right time to dwell on being between her legs when I have more pressing problems to figure out.

I knock on the door, and not long after, Cruz answers with a surprised face.

"What are you doing here?"

"Mom told me Addison wanted this manuscript," I lie, keeping my expression flat. "Is she here? I can't exactly leave it lying around."

Cruz snorts, turning back around as I follow him. "Yeah, because I care what's inside the smutty books."

"The smutty books, as you refer to them, bring in high revenue. The profit on these books makes the company wealthy, and that's how Mom and Dad paid for your college tuition."

A laugh escapes Cruz. "So, I should be thanking the dirty old women for putting me through college?"

"Never mind," is all I say, ignoring his immaturity. "So, what time do you expect Addison home?"

Cruz shrugs, plonking himself on the couch. "You tell me, bro. She only told me a few hours ago she's going out with some guy. I've sent her multiple texts, but she's not responding."

I nod then sit beside him. "I can wait so that Mom gets off my back."

"The woman is a ballbreaker sometimes."

"Try working with her."

Ten minutes pass, and the entire time, Cruz plays his game with a string of profanities expelling from his loud mouth when he's close to losing. I check the time on my phone again, noting it's after nine. *Fucking late for a date.*

Carefully, I tilt my phone, so Cruz can't see my screen.

ME

Are you having fun on your date?

I wait five minutes, the message showing unread. The rise in my body temperature is causing a headache as my patience grows thin for each minute that passes. Who the hell does she think she is? Going on a date and doing God knows what.

Don't go there.

My fingers type before the words even form a sentence in my head.

ME

Answer me.

Then, there's a rattle at the door and laughter coming from the other side. The door opens suddenly to Addison's bright face with all smiles, falling the moment she sees me.

"Addy," Cruz greets while eyeing the guy beside her. He's tall, but not as tall as me. Dressed in a pair of jeans and tee, very casual considering it's a date. "Why didn't you pick up your phone?"

She forces a smile. "Because I was at dinner with Harrison."

The guy extends his hand to shake Cruz's. "You must be the roommate."

Cruz returns the gesture, but his expression is less than friendly, and Mom's conversation from earlier comes to mind. "Her best friend as well."

Then, Harrison turns his attention to me, extending his hand. I reluctantly shake it, then pull away as quickly as possible.

"Masen's my brother," Cruz mumbles, but his annoyance is evident. "So, why did you guys come back here?"

"Just to show him around, you know," she trails off.

There's a momentary silence before Cruz scratches his head and looks at me.

"I'm starving," he complains. "Guess you guys have eaten. I might grab some Indian, although the guy, Raj, likes to small talk, and I'm fresh out of topics."

"I'll come with you," Harrison offers, "I spent a year in India, so my Hindu isn't so bad."

"Are you sure? I can come with you guys?" Addison asks, almost panicked.

"Actually, why don't you stay," I tell her. "Mom mentioned some stuff about this manuscript she wanted your feedback on."

When Addison walks toward the kitchen, Cruz and Harrison begin to walk to the door. The moment the door shuts behind them, I follow her, leaning against the the wall with my arms folded beneath my chest.

She continues to ignore me, staring into the refrigerator. I do my best to control my temper, biting down on my lip to calm myself as much as possible.

"Okay, since you won't talk. I'll ask the question again. Why were you on a date?"

Addison turns to face me with wild eyes. "You don't call or message me for one whole week. I'm not sure why you deserve an answer, Masen. By how things were left off between us, I assume you have moved on."

"So, is that why you went on a date?"

"It wasn't a date," she argues, turning away.

"Did you fuck him?"

Her gaze snaps in my direction as she lets out a forceful breath. "I'm not that type of woman. Contrary to what you may think, I don't sleep around. What happened between us was a mistake. It's done, and maybe you should leave before your brother hears us arguing."

She turns her back toward me, and without even thinking, I take steps to move in closer. When she's trapped between the refrigerator and me, she closes the door with a sigh.

"Masen," she barely whispers. "Let's not do this, please."

I don't listen, knowing she wants me to touch her. Goosebumps cover her skin, and I can almost smell the arousal between her legs. I slide my hands beneath her skirt and thrust my fingers inside her, not giving her a chance to pull away.

Addison places her hands on the stainless-steel door, glancing at the front door in a panic. She's crumbling beneath my touch, riding my fingers just like she would my cock.

"Did you think going on a date with another man was a smart idea?" I demand to know as she bites her tongue, not saying a word. "Answer me, Addison."

"I don't belong to you."

My fingers go in deeper at the same time she attempts to swallow and silence her moan.

"Is that so? So, you don't care if I fuck other women? Make their pussy come all over my pierced cock?"

In a sudden move, she grabs my wrist and pulls my fingers out, swiftly turning around so we're face-to-face.

"Don't do this."

"Do what, exactly?"

"Try to make me jealous."

"Well," I say, running my thumb against her bottom lip. "You had no problem making me jealous, now did you?"

"I hate you right now," she tells me with fire in her eyes. "I hate that I want you and all you'll give me is sex."

"I never said that, Addison."

"Then why didn't you call or text?"

"Why didn't you?" I counter.

"Because I'm not that girl."

"Right, so to clarify. You don't sleep around with men. You're not clingy. You don't believe in friends-with-benefits. Am I missing something?"

Addison bows her head, shaking it softly. "You can't possibly understand."

I place my finger beneath her chin and raise it so our eyes meet.

"What do you want from me, Addison?"

"I don't know, okay? All I know is that the last week has been hard."

My gaze lingers on her lips. "It's been hard for me too."

Then, she lifts her eyes but quickly glances sideways to the door. Her hand grabs my wrist again, directing me between her legs.

"You're not finished."

A smirk plays on my lips as I lick them with delight. "If I make you come, then it's only me who gets to touch you like this, you understand?"

Addison clutches my shirt with both her hands, bringing me in for a deep kiss.

"And if I come, then no one else touches you, deal?"

I kiss her back with force, racing against my heart which pounds inside my chest. What we're doing is dangerous.

But for now, no one else will touch what's deemed to be mine. And I'll make damn sure it stays this way.

FIFTEEN

ADDISON

"Do you want me to finish or not?"

I'm lying on my stomach, attempting to go through the manuscript for book two. If it weren't for the distraction beside me, I'd have binge-read the book in a matter of hours. In the space of ten minutes, I've re-read the same line three times. Considering it's a sex scene, it should be easy to read but I've lost track of exactly where the character's hands are positioned, and what he's doing with his tongue.

"But you're naked, and I can't concentrate," Masen complains with a devious smile, knowing full well I'm trying to read.

"I've been naked all night. In fact, you said if I gave you a blow job, you'd leave me alone. I held up my end of the bargain, but clearly, you have not."

"Fine," he sulks, falling onto his back and removing his hands from me.

The loss of his touch is hard to bear, but I try my best to ignore the momentary loss in an effort to finish this story. I'm over halfway, and of course, the author throws in a plot twist that has made my stomach turn upside down. I pause for a moment, reflecting on the past week and how things changed between Masen and me the night when I went out with Harrison.

We'd gone as far as to admit our time apart was hard, and the jealousy drove us both to do things out of character. So, for the past week, we did the opposite—we've been with each other almost every day.

The juggling act, however, proves difficult for me. I dedicated the little spare time I had between my studies and work to him. Masen's penthouse has become our refuge or lair of lovemaking if being more accurate. Damn, too much Eric. He'd be proud of me if he knew.

It's the only place where we have privacy and freedom to do whatever we please.

And that we did.

Masen is insatiable in the bedroom.

I'd meet him after work, without having dinner yet, only for him to ravage me the second I walked through the door. To set the record straight, I never complained. Since the strenuous workout left me famished, we always ate a big meal afterward. But eating big equates to a food coma, which resulted in me crashing here several times. When I woke in the middle of the night, Masen refused to let me leave. It wasn't worth the argument, so I ended up each time falling asleep in his arms.

It wasn't a problem the first time, but then Cruz began asking more questions. The more I'm away from home, the more he demands my attention when I'm there.

And this juggling act I found myself in is becoming difficult to balance. I found myself lying to protect him, only to be riddled with guilt afterward. It isn't the right time to say anything because I know our friendship will be compromised once he finds out. Cruz has always been sensitive over his relationship with Masen, and this won't go down well at all.

For now, Masen and I are having fun. No definitions, just fun.

"I'm feeling sick over this plot twist. Please don't tell me she chooses the other guy?"

Masen is lying beside me with his chest exposed. He purposely ignores me with a mischievous grin while typing on his phone. I'm drawn once again to how sexy he is beside me, sensing the familiar tingle travel through my body from just looking at his.

It's the little things, like the way his dark brown hair is messy and falls to the side of his face. And how when he smiles, there's a really small dimple on his left cheek. Then, there's the stubble on his sharp jawline—masculine and so sexy— and quite odd since facial hair on women is just the opposite.

I place the manuscript down, needing a break to relieve my eyes, but truth be told—I need to feel him inside me, now. I'm greedy, selfish—and chances are he won't complain.

My hand runs along the contour of his abs, tracing them delicately. Beneath the white bedsheet, his cock hardens, which is the perfect time to strike.

"You're distracting me," he cites with a hint of sarcasm in his voice.

"Hmm ... what am I distracting you from?"

"Hooking up with chicks on Tinder."

I smack him with my hand. "You're such a liar. As if you're on Tinder?"

The cocky grin on his face does nothing to slow down my desire to have him. I grab his phone to see him playing some word game on the screen.

"Ah, I knew you were a geek," I deadpan. "Tinder my ass."

He places his phone down. "Are you jealous?"

"No, I just knew you weren't on Tinder because women fall at your feet like all the time. With how you look, you don't need no sex app."

"Is that so, Miss Edwards?"

I nod. "You can't tell me there hasn't been any woman trying to hook up with you in the last week?"

Masen bows his head, falling quiet. I sit up with a sudden awareness of my heart beating a little too fast this time.

"There is?"

"Yes, but I have not responded to a single one of them."

"I can't believe you," I mutter in annoyance. "Show me the texts."

"I'd rather not."

My arms cross beneath my chest, trying to suppress my anger. A simple joke has now turned into this—my jealousy taking over and making me think crazy things.

"Show me," I demand again.

"You'll get angry even though I haven't responded to a single one of them."

A light bulb clicks in my head, reverse psychology. All I need to do is make him think he needs to prove himself in order to show me what those messages say.

"Since you won't show me, I kind of don't believe you. Maybe I should go..."

He shoves the phone at me. "Fine, here."

I gladly take it from him as he tells me which messages are from these so-called women. My eyes widen at what these women—three, to be exact—have sent him. The first woman, Jennifer, sent him a dirty text saying how perfect his pierced cock is and how she needs it in her mouth again. As each word passes, the blood inside my veins rises.

The second message is from Victoria. She sent a link to a

pornographic video with the thumbnail showing a woman squirting in some guy's face. *Is he into this?*

Then, the last text is from Jorja. It's a video of her rubbing her pussy while calling his name. I only watch the first few seconds before hitting stop. In silence, I toss the phone back and slide down, so I'm staring at the ceiling, trying to calm the jealousy inside me, which has consumed any rational thoughts trying to break through.

"Addison," he says softly. "They're nothing."

"They're not nothing. These women want you."

"Yes, but I don't want them. The only person I want is lying beside me looking all sexy because she's jealous."

"It's not funny," I scold him. "How would you like it if men sent me stuff like that?"

"I wouldn't like it. Correction, I'd hate it and probably call each one of those fuckers and threaten to end their life."

"So, you know..."

The bed shuffles as he climbs on top of me. His hazel eyes are staring intensely into my own, willing my heart to slow down at the touch of his finger on my lips.

"I want you, Addison. That's all you need to know."

I release a sigh. "I thought you hated me. Hence, the hate fucking."

The corners of his lips curve upward into a smile. "I've never hated you. But I'll admit you ignoring me almost all our lives does rile a reaction from me."

"So, if I'm analyzing this correctly, you've been secretly in love with me for all these years but pretended to despise me. Just like the boy in the schoolyard who teases the girl to get her attention?"

His eyes drift sideways, only for me to realize the words *in love* are probably an exaggeration of how he feels—a big one at that.

"I'm sorry," I apologize, shaking my head. "I didn't mean love in such a strong sense."

Masen's gaze anchors mine, kickstarting the butterflies inside my stomach to flutter in anticipation.

"What we're doing, Addison..." he begins with, pausing to think about his words, "...is something I've never done before. I've fucked women, lots of them. But that's the extent of it. You, inside my bed, this is different."

My stare falls onto his lips, then slowly, I plant a soft kiss. "Sometimes, different is good."

He returns the kiss, causing me to moan softly into his mouth. "I agree. Different is good."

"So back to these messages of yours..."

His lips taste mine again, this time with a raw passion ready to be unleashed.

"As I said, jealousy looks hot on you."

Just as I'm about to open my mouth and voice my annoyance, he spreads my thighs apart and enters me without warning. I gasp at the sensation, throwing my head back into the pillow. He pumps into me, nice and slow, burying his head in the crook of my neck while sucking on my skin. At the same time, he roughly squeezes my breast, causing me to moan loudly.

It's not long before I warn him of my impending orgasm, and just like every time we fuck, he demands we come together.

The sensations rip throughout me as my entire body shudders in a euphoric state. His grunts follow, then he collapses on my body from the exhaustion.

"Okay, maybe I was jealous," I admit, trying to catch my breath. "I know you didn't respond, but I don't like other women messaging you with such dirty content."

"Would you like me to tell them the only pussy I want to be inside belongs to Addison Edwards?"

"Sure," I muse, with a nod and wide grin. "I'm sure that screenshot will go down well with my father after he sees it broadcasted on TMZ."

"Speaking of Lex..."

I release a groan even before he says a word. "What has my father done now?"

"Your father has done nothing but invite me to his house for your mother's birthday. Sorry, correction. Eric forced him to invite everyone to his house for your mother's birthday."

"Oh yeah," I mumble, remembering the panicked text from Eric since it's so last-minute and Mom has no clue. "Mom hates surprise birthday parties. She once told me, Eric threw her a party pre-married to Dad days. She said it was so awkward because at the time, she was engaged to Uncle Julian and Dad was unstoppable in his pursuit for Mom. She said Dad was so jealous that she drank so much sangria, and the next day had the worst hangover of her life."

Masen chuckles softly. "Sounds like your dad."

My finger traces his shoulder blade as questions plague me.

"So, do you spend much time with my dad?"

He pulls himself out of me, collapsing next to where I lay. "Why do you ask?"

"Just curious."

"I do, actually. He's a stakeholder in Lantern Publishing, a shark in the boardroom if you cross him, and also the one who tames my dad when the men go out."

This time, it's my turn to laugh. "Your dad needs taming? No..."

"Haden Cooper needs a leash on him."

"So, what you're really trying to tell me is that the apple doesn't fall far from the tree?"

Masen digs his finger into my ribs, making me jump from being ticklish.

"Despite what my mother likes to tell people, I'd like to think I'm the apple who found his own feet and works hard without needing his parents to push him."

I nod in agreement. "From what I overhear, you're a workaholic—"

The sound of his phone pings, stopping me mid-sentence. He drags his phone to look at a text, then laughs.

In annoyance, I roll my eyes. "Another booty text?"

"Your sister."

My eyes widen in shock. "My sister sends you booty texts?"

Masen frowns. "God, no. Ava is like an annoying sister who has your back, but at the same time, you're adamant she was put on this earth to push every button you have. We're still arguing over sandwich etiquette."

The tension in my shoulders releases, knowing it's just Ava being Ava.

"If you really want to annoy her, tell her in Denmark, the sandwiches are open-faced with roast beef and fish fillets."

"She has an aversion to mixed meats." He chuckles.

"Exactly... target her triggers."

As he begins to type, I snatch the phone off him and type my own message.

MASEN

> In Denmark, they serve open-faced sandwiches with roast beef and fish fillets. It's not uncommon to throw in some egg. Sounds tasty, right?

The bubble appears, then the phone beeps.

AVA

> WHAT THE HELL IS WRONG WITH YOU?

> There's no place in the world for roast beef and fish together. I think I just threw up in my mouth. I'm not talking to you for the rest of the day.

> Goodbye.

We both laugh at Ava's response. Her reactions are priceless if you know how to push her buttons.

"And that's how you get my sister to stop annoying you," I conclude.

"It was so easy, too. I'll learn a lot from you."

"Hmm," I murmur while shifting to climb on top of him. The sheet falls off, exposing my breasts. "I'm wondering what else I can teach you."

Masen places his hands on my hips, grinding against me until he's hard again. This man will be the death of me.

"We've got all night."

"Sleep is overrated, anyway."

"Sleep?" he questions, tilting his head. I slide myself on, watching his face tense in delight. "You'll be the death of me, Miss Edwards."

"Exactly my words," I say with a sly smile, gently rocking back and forth at a teasing pace. "Are you ready for me again?"

He places his arm behind his head with eyes full of lust. "Ride me, cowgirl."

SIXTEEN

ADDISON

"**W**here the party at, bruh!"

Rocky's grand entrance is not without the usual chaos he brings when he knows the night will end up with him drunk and in an argument with Nikki.

He drops his hands from the air, spinning around in a burgundy-purple velvet suit with leather lapels paired with white leather shoes. I have to give it to him, he doesn't look his age, and if perusing a club, I'm sure he can pass for a much younger man.

That's if he kept his big mouth shut.

"Where's the birthday girl?" he announces with a huge grin, extending his arms to hug Mom. "Papa has a gift for you."

Eric scowls. "I'm equally disgusted and turned on by you calling yourself Papa."

"It's this new thing he's trying," Nikki drags. "Just like when he went through the big daddy stage."

"Better than Papi Chulo," Mom complains. "I knew

going to Spanish class at your age would have adverse effects."

"I wanted to expand my linguistic knowledge," Rocky defends with a smirk. "So when we traveled, I didn't look like a dick and order the wrong food again. My ass hugged the toilet bowl all night long after eating that dish."

Aunt Adriana overhears when she walks in with Uncle Julian. "So it had nothing to do with the young twins with the double Ds?"

"Are we back to fantasizing about twins again?" Nikki huffs.

"Baby, why would I want twins when I have you?"

I shudder, knowing something is about to be said that I don't want to hear. My sisters are over by the food, devouring everything and blaming the post-pregnancy hormones again. Quietly, I walk over to them and leave Rocky trying to defend himself.

"Is it safe to stay here?" Millie asks, frowning. "Rocky looks like he's telling a story, and I've heard way too much. I'm not sure whether I'm supposed to be fortunate or unlucky in the father-in-law department."

"Unlucky," Will contests with annoyance. "Try growing up with him."

Ava snorts. "Oh really? Try growing up with Lex Edwards as your father and tell me if that's easier."

Will rubs his chin with a dismissive glance. "Try sleeping with his daughter behind his back and almost losing everything you've worked your entire life for."

"You guys," I butt in, trying not to roll my eyes at them. "This isn't a competition. You both have loving fathers who are your family no matter what. So they've got their quirks, big deal."

Arms wrap around my waist, prompting me to smile until I realize it's not the arms I've grown accustomed to wrapping around my naked body. My hands clutch onto his wrists as I turn around to face Cruz.

"You're here," I greet, a little too high-pitched, which makes it sound like I'm surprised. "I thought you were coming later?"

"The meeting finished earlier than expected," he simply replies.

"Oh, how did it go?"

Cruz scratches the back of his neck. "We'll talk about it later."

My attention shifts to Haden and Presley walking out the large back patio doors, and right behind them is the one person I've been waiting for.

Masen.

His stride is so masculine, filled with confidence in every step he takes. Slowly, he lifts his gaze while running his hand through his hair. Then, the hazel eyes burn into my soul, igniting every inch of my body.

It's been four days since I saw him last because his work got in the way. With all the acquisitions Lantern Publishing is going through now, he was called to travel and hasn't been home. We resorted to texting, but nothing compares to seeing him in the flesh.

My dad stops him, shaking his hand, forcing him to turn away. I lower my gaze to the floor, staring at my feet because the truth is bubbling to the surface, and I'm not sure how long I can deny it.

I missed him.

"Addison," Presley calls my name. "We need to talk."

"We do?" I choke in a panic. "About what?"

"The manuscript for part two. Masen said you were reading it and finished. I need your feedback because I have some concerns."

"Um, sure. I thought Masen had read it too. Don't you want his feedback?"

Presley pats my arm while laughing. "I got his feedback which surprised me. He's not a romance reader, so his opinion is usually one-sided, but he had a lot more to say this time."

Ava is standing beside us, overhearing our conversation. "Yeah, something is up with him lately. Maybe he's in love or something."

I choke on my saliva, letting out an impromptu cough.

"Are you okay?" Ava asks, patting my back.

"Yeah, sorry, your comment was just shocking. As if he'd fall in love. The guy's a player." I press my lips flat. "Sorry, Presley."

"Please, I know he is, but I agree with Ava. Someone's gotten to him." Presley leans in at the same time Ava and I do. "I found a t-shirt at his place when he asked me to let the maintenance guy in. It was a woman's shirt. He never lets any woman stay over. It's his rule, according to Haden."

Ava laughs. "Oh, this is getting interesting. I mean, he's been moody but also extra chatty at the same time. Tell us what's on the shirt so we can figure out what type of girl she is."

My breaths are quick and shallow, my heart palpitating with tingling inside my chest. *Please don't say what's on the shirt, I beg silently.*

"There was a pineapple on the front wearing glasses, and it's reading a book." Presley describes the shirt perfectly, but maybe if I'm lucky, Ava won't remember.

If I'm lucky.

And the universe is on my side.

"How funny!" Ava blurts out while laughing. "If you wear pineapples on a shirt, it means you're into swinging. It's like a swinging code in public. Last Christmas, I bought ..."

Ava's eyes widen at the same time her mouth falls open. "What is it, Ava?"

"Um..." she stumbles with a shaky breath. "I've seen those shirts around a lot. What color was it?"

"Like a pinkish salmon color," Presley informs her.

I keep my face blank, forcing a smile until Ava swivels her head at a slow and agonizing pace like those creepy dolls you see in horror movies.

"Presley, would you excuse Addy and me? I forgot I have to show her something upstairs for the baby."

"Of course. We'll talk later, Addison." Presley glances at Haden, who's laughing with Rocky. "That laughter sounds dirty. I better brace myself."

There's not even a second to breathe before Ava grabs my arm and drags me through the party. From where Masen stands, he spots her taking me inside. He keeps his expression blank until I widen my eyes and press my lips so he can hopefully read my face.

Ava doesn't stop at the kitchen, dragging me to her bedroom. The moment the door closes, she lets go.

"Are you kidding me, Addy?" she shouts with a judgmental stare.

I cross my arms beneath my chest. "I have no idea what you're talking about."

"You're fucking Masen."

"Ava, you're ridiculous."

"Um, hello! The shirt?" she accuses with an unrelenting stare. "That shirt was custom made. I gave it to you at Christmas as a joke because of the whole swingers' thing. It was made in salmon color because that's one of our favorite scenes in the show *Friends.*"

Before I respond, my phone vibrates in my pocket. I quickly pull it out to see a message from Masen.

MASEN

> Please don't tell me you told Ava. Fucking hell Addison.

Ava yanks the phone off me to read the message.

"Ava! That's my phone."

She hits dial and places the call on speaker. When he picks up, Ava is quick to yell, "Come to my room now, young man."

I lower my head, still refusing to answer her question. Several minutes later, the door opens, and Masen steps in. I can't look his way, ready for the wrath of my older sister.

Ava's eyes dart between us. "So, who would like to start?"

"It's not what you think it is."

"I think my good friend, who I've known my entire life and is like a brother to me, is fucking my baby sister. Am I accurate enough?"

Masen pinches the bridge of his nose. "Can you not make a big deal of this?"

Ava gasps dramatically, typical of her to react this way. As for me, my butterflies are on the verge of vomiting from the stress of this night.

"Not make a big deal out of this?" she repeats in a high-pitched tone. "Addison doesn't just fuck men. So, if she does, it's a super big deal. Throw you into the mix, it's an even bigger deal. I don't understand. You guys loathe each other."

"Firstly, thanks for pointing out my sexual history. No, I don't just fuck men, Ava. I'm not you."

Ava's mouth falls open. "Exactly why this is the biggest deal ever. Are you in love with him?"

My heart stops beating at the mention of 'love.' I can't look at Masen, not wanting to freak out because Ava is losing the plot. Love is a strong word. You can't just say it when you feel like it without losing its importance.

"This isn't the biggest deal. A bigger deal was Millie

sleeping with Will. An even bigger deal was you having a one-night stand with your sister's ex-fiancé and getting pregnant," I remind her with animosity. "Don't make this bigger than it has to be. Yes, we're sleeping together, and that's it."

"Oh?" Ava nods with a forced smile, then turns to Masen. "And what about you? Are you only sleeping with Addison, or is she one of the many you're stringing along right now?"

"Ava," Masen grits, clenching his fists. "I'm trying my hardest to respect that you've just had a baby and are probably charging with hormones, but I'll say this once. This is mine and Addison's business, not yours. To set the record straight, I haven't been with anyone since this began. That's all I'll say on this."

Ava shakes her head in disbelief. "I can't believe you two. So, what now? Are you telling Mom and Dad? Is this gonna end up in marriage? What if you get knocked up? Oh my god, I can't handle Dad getting all alpha angry again."

"You need to calm down, okay? Mom and Dad don't need to know. And please stop talking about nonsense stuff. Give me some credit. You know how I feel about marriage. I'm not you or Millie."

"Fine. I'm going to step outside to give you some privacy to discuss how you're going to walk outside and pretend I don't know anything. I'll be at the end of the hall to make sure no one comes here." Ava raises her hand and points her finger at me, then Masen. "Do not have sex in my room, you understand?"

"Oh sure," I drag, rolling my eyes. "But it was okay for you to have sex with Austin downstairs in the cellar on Christmas Eve? Do you know Mom and Dad have sex in there? It's like a sex dungeon."

"I did no such thing."

"The cameras didn't lie."

"You watched me?!"

"Alexa ..."

"Fuck," she mumbles beneath her breath.

"You can thank our baby sister for deleting the footage before Dad saw it."

Ava's cheeks turn bright red as she lowers her gaze and quietly exits the room, closing the door behind her.

Masen is pacing Ava's room, making the silence uncomfortable. Not once have we discussed telling our families, knowing everyone will have an opinion. It doesn't seem right when I don't even have my own opinion yet. Everything between us is new, and I'm still trying to process it all.

"I don't know what to say."

"Maybe we should just tell everyone," he suggests with frustration.

My eyes snap to meet his deep stare. "Tell them what, exactly? That we're sleeping together?"

"That we're seeing each other."

"Which everyone will think we're just fucking since you're not one to be in a relationship."

"And neither are you," he argues back.

My pulse races, fueled by anger. "I don't have a reputation for sleeping around."

"Why do you care what other people think?"

"I care, okay!"

"Right, what you really care about is hurting my brother," he lowers his voice, but I hear the resentment just as loud. "Just admit it."

"Of course, I don't want to hurt Cruz."

"So this boils down to my brother and me. That's my competition."

I throw my hands up in the air. "There's no competition. I'm not in love with Cruz."

The second it leaves my mouth, Masen stills his movements. I turn away, unable to look at him as my muscles clench and my breath is caught in my throat.

"We should go," I say faintly. "Before someone sees or hears us."

I leave the room first and walk past Ava, not stopping to say anything. My feet move quickly outside, straight to my parents' bar where Uncle Julian is serving drinks. When he's designated bartender, you know Nikki is involved. He makes Rocky think he's drinking shots but waters down the liquor to avoid him getting blind drunk.

"Addison," he greets me with a warm smile. "Soda?"

"Tequila."

He cocks his head. "The hard stuff. Is everything okay?"

"It will be after a few shots."

The bottle comes out, and I down the first. We chat for a little bit about school until he willingly pours me another. Just as I'm about to drink the second, Dad joins me.

"We're not repeating the last event when you drank Haden under the table?"

I shake my head, pursing my lips. "I've been studying a lot this week."

Yeah, I studied Masen's body and how beautiful the man is naked. Am I in love with him? Fuck, why did I even mention the goddamn word?

Haden puts his arm around me. "Leave the girl alone. It's nice to find a drinking buddy."

I take the glass. At the same time, Haden demands Julian pour one for him and Dad. Once all three of us have one in our hand, we raise them in the air and cheer, then throw it back.

It should burn my throat, but the memory of what happened upstairs burns more.

The music is cranked up louder, courtesy of Rocky and Eric, who hit the make-shift dancefloor first. Uncle Noah and

Kate arrive late, having just landed from London. The two of them look tired but wanted to stop by to say happy birthday to Mom.

Masen spends most of his night with Will. Austin was called to work for an emergency, but Ava doesn't complain. My cousin Andy and Jessa were in Manhattan, unable to travel this week, but it isn't too bad since I'm visiting them next week.

Aunt Adriana and Presley bring out a big cake with candles as we all sing happy birthday to Mom. Dad stands beside her with glassy eyes, knowing Haden has gotten his way once again.

I have to admit, Dad is fun when he's drunk, which is rare these days.

The dancefloor picks up again, but I'm not in the mood. Ava keeps her distance from me, hanging out with Mille. Alexa is sitting with my cousins Willow and Sienna. Luna is away for the weekend in Cabo with some old dude, according to Ava. Ava's sources are so shady I highly doubt it's true.

There's a pair of hands resting on my hips, but then they fall off as Cruz grabs my hand and drags me to the dancefloor. Even though I'm not in the mood, I dance for a few minutes to get him off my back.

As he wraps his arms around my waist to bring me in, he leans in to whisper. "I've missed you, Addy."

I smack his chest. "What are you talking about, you goof? I've been around."

"No, you haven't. You've been out a lot with friends."

My feet continue to dance, but I'm unsure of what to say. "You know how it is."

Cruz places his hand on the small of my back while stilling his movements. He leans in again, but across the dancefloor, Masen watches me with a jealous stare.

"Can we talk tonight, please?"

I'm distracted by Masen's tight grip on the glass he holds, to the way his jaw is clenching. His stare is tight, unrelenting, and full of rage.

"Sure," I tell him, then remove Cruz's hands from my back. "I need to use the restroom."

I don't wait for him to respond, walking fast toward my bedroom for some solitude. Most of my family are drunk enough not to notice I'm gone, aside from Ava, who side-eyes me as I'm walking away.

The house is quiet, the silence welcoming to slow down my racing thoughts. I reach my room, letting out a sigh when the familiar surroundings wash over me with a sense of calm.

Just as I'm about to close the door, a hand pushes through. I'd recognize those hands anywhere. They've been all over my body and traced every inch of my skin.

"Addison," Masen breathes.

"Not now. I need to be alone."

He grabs my wrist, pulling me toward him. Our lips crash together, and the spark between us ignites like dynamite ready to explode. I begin to grow feverish from the taste of his lips on mine, but I pull back, knowing my thoughts are jumbled, and I don't want to say another thing I regret.

Masen's breathing is ragged, his gaze fixated on my mouth as he traces my bottom lip with his thumb. My skin shivers in delight, warning me I need to stop him or else we're in trouble.

I can do this.

Just say *no*.

"I've missed you," he whispers, then places a soft kiss on my lips.

And in just three words, my world is shining in a different light.

In just a short matter of time, I've fallen in love with him.

A man I've spent my whole life avoiding.

SEVENTEEN

MASEN

"I've missed you."

My lips caress hers with a sense of calm.

Inside Addison's room, the music from outside drowns in the background. There is loud singing, no doubt coming from Rocky and Eric.

But the only thing I can focus on is the beautiful woman in front of me who inadvertently admitted she's in love with me.

The four-letter word caught me by surprise. After Ava's unnecessary interrogation, which involved talk about marriage, my nerves have been anything but calm all night. I shouldn't be so surprised by Ava's reaction. She's dramatic at the best of times, and she knows me well. I'm not one to hold a relationship and choose to sleep around for my own selfish needs.

Yet, with Addison, it's entirely different.

My emotions were a train wreck when it came to her. I hadn't seen her the last four days because of work, unable to concentrate in meetings or even sleep at night inside the lonely hotel room. No matter what I do, I can't escape my need to have her inside my bed where it's only us.

Then, I see my brother touch her on the dancefloor. I was this close to walking up and punching the fucker until Dad noticed and calmed me down. I should feel sorry for the guy. He's caught between two sons. But what do I care? All I want is Addison to be mine and none of this bullshit sneaking around anymore.

As we stand in her room, I want nothing more than to strip her down to nothing on her childhood bed. This sick fantasy of mine is possible if we just lock the door and turn off the lights.

Addison releases a sigh, placing her hands on my chest. "I've missed you too, but we can't be caught here."

"I know."

"About earlier ..."

"We don't need to talk about it now," I tell her.

"We don't?"

My lips find hers again, but this time, I roll my tongue to taste her better. Fuck, I'm getting hard from just a kiss. It's only been four fucking days, so why does it feel like I haven't touched her since eternity.

"There's something I'd rather do to occupy the small amount of time we have in here."

I bury my head in her neck, spreading kisses on her skin as she moans in delight.

"We can't, not here."

"Then where else?" I ask while still sucking on her delicate skin.

"Your place, later tonight."

"I'm not waiting that long," I inform her.

"If someone catches us—"

I place my hand over her mouth then use my other hand to take her to the bathroom. I close the door and lock it behind us when we're inside. My hand falls, but then I push her against the vanity, pressing my cock into her ass.

The mirror hangs over the vanity with our reflection. Addison is wearing a black leather skirt and boots, something I've been eyeing all night.

My hand slides up her skirt, then I yank her panties down.

"I want you to watch me as I fuck you," I whisper in her ear.

As I'm about to grab my cock to enter her, she pushes my hand aside and does it herself. Her soft hand cradling my shaft feels fucking amazing. Slowly, she guides me in, and I feel her pussy clench on my hard cock. *Fuck, she feels like heaven.*

Instead of gripping her hips, my hand sits at the base of her neck. My body moves on its own accord, relishing in the pure ecstasy of being inside her. Every thrust is pushing me over the edge, and it's not long before Addison will warn me she's just about to come.

"How do we look?" I ask, watching our reflection.

"Like two people who were always meant to be together," she murmurs, throwing her head back in delight. I tighten my grip on her neck, forcing her to look at the mirror again. "It's only you, Masen. I promise it's only you to ever fuck me this way."

Her words are like dynamite, fueling my possessive need to own her. I don't give a fuck what anyone says. No other man will go near her. Not for as long as I shall breathe.

I slow my movements but stay inside her. The reflection is just the two of us, caught in this forbidden moment. Her eyes search mine, and behind the desire, there's nothing left but to admit the truth.

"Addison, I need to own you."

She laces her arm behind my neck, bringing me in closer. "Then own me."

I wrap her hair around my hand while moving inside her again. My lips ravage her neck, but as desired, my gaze flicks back to our reflection as we ride the wave together and I come inside her.

My body shudders as she clenches all over me. The warm sensation spreads all over my cock, causing me to tighten my grip on her. Our breathing echoes inside the bathroom, but given we're in her parents' house, I don't linger and pull myself out.

We both clean ourselves up in silence, knowing time is not on our side. I reach for her arm to pull her close to me.

"If you want to talk tonight, we can talk at my place."

A smile graces her perfect pink lips, the emerald in her eyes shining bright.

"You're always distracted at your place. Unless it's dirty talk."

"I won't argue that," I say, running my hand down her cheek. "But you'll stay with me tonight?"

"Of course."

I leave her room first but opt to take a different route to outside. I've spent a lot of my childhood inside this house, so I know every single room and where the halls lead to. However, the last thing I need now is to be caught by Lex.

Just before I step onto the main patio, I run into Ava. Closing my eyes momentarily, I muster the patience to deal with her right now.

"Look, I'm sorry about before. It caught me by surprise and to find out in front of your mom."

I tilt my head in confusion. "My mom?"

"She mentioned how you've changed and how she found a woman's shirt at your place. When she explained what the shirt looked like, I put two-and-two together."

"Right, the pineapple shirt," I mumble.

"Masen, my sister isn't a relationship girl. Don't hurt her."

"Hurt Addison?" I repeat, crossing my arms over my chest. "I'm not the one caught in the middle of two brothers."

"C'mon, Addison doesn't look at Cruz that way..."

The moment it leaves Ava's mouth, laughter catches our attention. We both shift our gaze to where Rocky has started a bonfire. Addison sits down on the patio bench as Cruz sits beside her, placing his arm around her. He continually leans in, whispering something to Addison, making her laugh.

My gaze sinks, then rips away from watching the two of them. "Tell me who's going to get hurt in the end, huh?"

"Addison would never hurt you. She's not capable of hurting anyone," Ava says with conviction.

Ava may think she knows her sister so well, but as my eyes drift back to them, what I'm seeing is something entirely different.

Cruz wants Addison for an entirely different reason.

"Let's go sit down before I pass out from exhaustion."

Ava laces her arm in mine, a simple move that catches Addison's attention. We sit across from them, near Lex and Charlie. Amelia is resting her head against Will, looking equally as tired on my other side. I'm not surprised, given the two of them have young babies. According to Ava, all their kids were being babysat by Austin's parents tonight since these parties tend to get out of control.

Rocky passes out, snoring loudly. Eric is also yawning as he speaks. Everyone is tired from a night of drinking and dancing.

"I'm getting old," Eric complains, letting out an even more prolonged yawn. "My party days are over."

Addison shakes her head with a laugh. "You're such a liar. You go out every weekend."

"True." Eric nods in agreement. "There's straight partying, and there's homosexual partying."

"And the difference being?" Charlie asks.

"No one here is wearing a fluorescent pink thong."

"Thank God," Cruz drags, then chuckles. "Maybe you ladies wouldn't look so bad."

"My son, everybody," Mom muses. "Blame Haden for that."

"Hey, one day, he'll settle down with a ball and chain. Let him live a little," Dad jests.

Cruz pulls Addison closer to him as I watch their bodies touch. The tightness inside my chest returns, crippling my ability to breathe at a normal pace. For every moment which passes, my fists clench tighter as the surge of anger is threatening to unleash.

"I've made a deal with Addy," Cruz mentions with pride. "If we're not married by thirty, we marry each other."

"We made that deal when we were eighteen, and I felt sorry for you because your ex broke your heart," Addison reminds him. "You were crying like a baby and said you'd never find love again."

"I love you, so why not?" Cruz turns to Lex with a grin. "I'm asking your permission, Lex. You're all good with this, right?"

"My daughter is a smart woman who's capable of making her own decisions. So, the answer is no," Lex informs him with a smirk.

Everyone laughs, but not me. Dad glances over with a concerned expression, then quickly forces a smile. Beside me, Ava's laugh is fake, trying not to appear obvious.

And across the bonfire, Addison's profound stare speaks a thousand words.

She's made commitments to my brother, and someone is bound to get hurt whichever way she follows.

People begin to leave, starting with Will and Amelia. Nikki follows with Will and Lex forced to carry a heavy Rocky to the car.

Mom offers to give me a lift, but I tell her I only had a few drinks and not enough to push me over the limit.

We all walk toward the front of the house, saying goodbye to each other. Cruz is standing beside Addison, only a few feet away, close enough for me to hear him talk.

"Let's go, Addy."

"Actually..." She lowers her gaze, then lifts it with a yawn. "I was going to crash here."

"Please?" Cruz begs. "I really want to talk to you."

"I'm tired, Cruz. Can't we talk tomorrow morning?"

My brother doesn't let up, and I'm this close to telling him to back the hell off. But once again, I'm forced to control myself in front of everyone not to make a scene.

"Addy, it's really important to me. I wouldn't beg if it weren't."

Addison's shoulders slump as she sighs dejectedly. "Okay, if it's important to you."

It's the nail in the coffin, the stab in the fucking heart.

She chose him... *again.*

I don't wait around for her to look at me, nor to stay another minute. Ava calls my name, but I don't bother to turn around. I fumble inside my pocket for my keys, pressing the button to unlock my car.

When I sit inside the driver's seat, I turn the ignition on and rev the engine to warm the car up. There's a tap on my window, and when I glance over, Dad motions for me to open the window.

I press the button, waiting for the window to slide down.

"Don't do anything stupid," he warns me.

My hands clutch the steering wheel, knuckles turning stark white. "Anything else?"

"You love her. That's why this hurts," Dad says in a low voice so no one can hear. "Don't jump into bed with someone else, thinking that will take away the pain. You do that. You'll lose her forever."

With a twisted mouth, I glance over to where my brother has his arm over the woman I love.

Love—what bullshit.

"She's going home with another man. I'm not the one breaking the rules, father."

And with that, I close the window and slam my foot on the accelerator to get the hell out of there.

My fingers trace the rim of the glass, slowly gliding against the smooth edge and eyeing the amber liquid with a desperate thirst. The bottle from the liquor cabinet is almost empty.

I'm sitting on my leather couch, remembering how Addison's naked body was lying on this very spot as I licked every inch of her pussy clean after blowing inside her.

The memories haunt me, refusing to leave no matter how hard I try to focus on anything else. My phone is beside me, but there's no message from her, or should I say no apology from her.

I scroll aimlessly, reading through my unread texts. An unopened text from Ariel is sitting inside my inbox. I open it, reading the lengthy message of exactly how she wants me to fuck her.

Dad's voice plays in my head.

"Don't jump into bed with someone else."

How can I jump into bed with someone else when my dick doesn't even stir at the dirty message sent to me? I'm fucking ruined, no chance of even getting hard for anyone else because Addison's got a hold of me.

A new text appears on my screen.

ANDY

Call me tomorrow when you can.

I hit dial without even thinking. The phone rings then he answers.

"Hey, Andy," I greet in a stiff tone. "It's late. Is everything okay?"

"Yeah, man. I just wanted to see if you're free to come to Manhattan next week. Jessa's book is launching, and since Lantern Publishing has everything to do with it, I want to make sure she takes a moment to celebrate her accomplishment."

"Of course," I tell him, blinking my eyes as my vision begins to blur. "Our management team has seen the numbers already. She's an orange flag bestseller without even releasing."

"It's been a long time coming. I'm proud she's finally doing this."

I shake my head with a grin, still in disbelief. Andy and Jessa are finally together and living in Manhattan. Only a few months ago, she was in London, living with her ex-husband. I'm glad Andy went after her. The guy has been in love with her since we were teens.

During my last visit to Manhattan, I managed to catch up for dinner with both of them. But the last few weeks have been chaotic with all my focus on Addison.

I take a deep breath, willing to rid my thoughts.

"So, when are you marrying the girl?" I ask him jokingly. "There are a few bets going around."

"Is that so?" Andy chuckles. "I'm proposing after dinner next week. Kind of planned something special."

"Congrats, man, just don't say anything to your cousins. They all have big mouths."

"Addy is probably the only one I can trust. I've texted her but haven't heard back. She must be busy with studying or her new job."

I bite my tongue because expressing my feelings to a good friend will only end in disaster. One accidental slip to Andy, and he'll probably tell Jessa. Then, the whole Edwards family will know.

"Yeah, I think Lex said she was busy."

"I might call her later. So, we're good for next week?"

"Wouldn't miss it, see you then."

We hang up the call, which prompts me to finish the remains inside the bottle. The final drop is tasteless, or perhaps I'm finally numb.

Not long after, my head begins to spin. I stumble toward my bed then fall face-first onto the pillow.

It smells just like her.

The pain stabs my chest directly in the center.

If this is what falling in love feels like, then I call bullshit.

I'm not going to be second best.

Not to a man who is my own flesh and blood.

EIGHTEEN

ADDISON

The drive back home is uneventful, and I'm consumed with guilt.

I heard the car screech off into the night, a sound charged with raw emotion which lingered well after it was gone.

The guilt ate away at me like a parasite feasting upon its prey because I'm responsible for the anger Masen is exhibiting. There wasn't a moment to explain to him why I felt forced to go home with Cruz. In the flash of an eye, he walked to his car and drove away without a goodbye.

My phone is resting in my hand, but I resist texting him in case he's still driving. If anything happened to Masen, I'd never be able to forgive myself.

Cruz presses the volume button and cranks up the music to drown out the silence. Usually, I'd argue and turn it down. Yet, the noise is a welcome distraction from the chaos going on inside my head.

At the apartment, the weight of tonight's events begins catching up to me. I let out a yawn, rubbing my eyes to stay awake. Then, I remember Cruz needs to talk. According to him, it's that important I needed to come home, and it can't wait until the morning.

"You wanted to talk?"

Sitting on the table is a bottle of gin. I hadn't noticed it earlier today, wondering where it came from. As I sit on one end of the couch, resting my elbow on the side to use it to support my tired head, Cruz unscrews the bottle and drinks straight from it.

He expels a rasp, then drinks more.

"You might want to slow down," I suggest.

Cruz paces the area in front of the coffee table, his nervous mannerisms piquing my curiosity. Suddenly, I begin to panic. What if something is wrong with him? He's not a shy guy at all, and our friendship has been built on honesty. *Yeah, except you've been dishonest of late.*

"So, um, at my meeting today, I've been requested to complete a physical and mental test for the coach and general manager of a top-winning team."

My eyes widen in surprise. "That's amazing, right? Wait, why don't you look happy?"

Cruz pauses, then aligns his gaze onto me. "It's in San Francisco."

I tilt my head in confusion. "And? That's only a short drive away."

Cruz moves toward the couch, sitting right next to me. He places his hand on mine as I wait for the story to unfold. Surely, there must be more to this. I knew he wanted to stay here, but San Francisco isn't that far either. At least, it's still in California.

"Addy, I can't leave you," he confesses in a low voice.

"Of course, you can leave me. I'm a big girl now. I mean, sure, I'll miss you, but we're talking about an opportunity most guys would die for."

"I... I think I'm in love with you."

My entire body freezes as the heaviness expands to my core. The tightness in my chest restricts my ability to breathe, causing my heart to still momentarily. Then, it begins to beat again—fast and erratic.

This can't be right. Maybe I heard the wrong words? Cruz is my best friend, and this isn't supposed to happen. I've trusted him with all my being and not with the intent for him to fall in love with me.

"I... I...," I stammer, unable to string together my words. "I don't understand how this happened."

"Do you have to understand how this happened? I'm in love with you, Addy. I can't lie to you anymore and pretend I don't feel this way."

"But this wasn't supposed to happen," I mumble while shaking my head. "We were always supposed to be best friends."

"Things change..."

His hand is still resting on top of mine. The warmth of skin is usually comforting in my time of need, but Cruz feels like a complete stranger right now. I pull my hand out from beneath his, quickly standing up and distancing myself.

"So, you don't want to follow your career because of me?" I question, running my hand through my hair. "Because you think you're in love with me?"

"I don't think," he states, bowing his head between his knees. "I know."

Just like he had done earlier, I pace in front of the coffee table. How did this happen? Were there signs? The last few weeks have been busy, and my head has been so clouded. Maybe it was all in front of me, but I was too occupied with his older brother at his sex lair doing all the dirty things.

A sharp pain spreads across my temple, an imminent headache warning me of its arrival.

"I need to go to bed and process this," I splutter, momentarily beyond words.

"Addy..."

I don't allow him to get another word in, desperate to escape him at this moment.

The door closes behind me, then I rest against it inside my room. My eyes close on their own accord, trying to process everything that just happened. My stomach is sick to its core, battling with my now headache, which causes me to wince in pain.

I walk over to the window, pulling the drapes shut so the morning light doesn't abuse me with its sunny rays. Then, I fall onto the bed and turn to the side, resting my hands beneath my head.

Tonight was too much.

I'm caught in this tangled web, unsure of how to climb my way out. No matter which direction I take, someone will get hurt. There are two significant men, and neither of them deserves to be hurt in any way, shape, or form.

I'm forced to close my eyes, my head now unbearable. Sleep is the only solution, and eventually, I drift off.

My head goes in and out of consciousness as my eyes slowly begin to open. The room is pitch black, but suddenly, the bed starts to move.

I let out a moan to feel a body move on top of me. *Where am I?* My limbs are weak, barely able to move. Then, lips press against mine. They're warm yet unfamiliar.

And they taste of gin.

My eyes snap open in a panic, realizing it's Cruz kissing me and not Masen. I press my hands on his chest, willing to push him away, but his strength outweighs me. The panic is soon overcome by anger, forcing me to turn my head to the right to break away from his lips.

"What the hell are you doing?" I question him angrily.

"Addy..." he moans, "... please give me this."

His intoxication fuels the desperation in his voice. I've been around him numerous times when he's had too much to drink, but not once has he ever tried to take advantage of me nor make a move to ruin what we have.

I manage to push him with force, then jump off the bed to distance myself.

"You do not get to come into my room and do that to me," I shout.

"Addy, don't—"

"I'm not staying here. I'll be at my parents' house."

In the dark, I grab my phone off the nightstand and run out to the hall, then through the apartment until I'm outside. I run down the stairs, out into the cool night, only to realize I left my car keys upstairs.

I can't call Mom or Dad to pick me up, knowing they had a fair bit to drink tonight. Instead, I call an Uber but walk down the street to the corner store to wait.

When the car arrives, I give my parents' address and send Mom a quick text.

ME

Mom, I'm coming back home tonight.

I don't expect her to respond, but the bubble appears and soon after a reply.

MOM

Okay, honey.

The driver pulls up to my parents' house. Thankfully, all the cars are gone, so only my parents and Alexa are home. I thank the driver, then step out and walk toward the main door. Punching in the code, the door opens. When I close it behind me, I notice all the lights are off besides a faint glow coming from down the long hallway.

I walk toward the kitchen to find Mom sitting by herself at the counter.

"Mom? Why are you awake."

"I wanted to clean up," she answers, but the worry is etched on her face. "Your father offered then passed out."

I nod then sit beside her.

"I'm here, Addy, if you want to talk or not talk."

My fingers become restless, scratching against my arms until my skin looks red raw.

"I don't know what to say…"

"Say everything or say nothing."

A heavy sigh escapes me. "Cruz told me he's in love with me."

Mom remains silent beside me. Then, she lets out a breath. "Are you surprised?"

My head swiftly turns to face her. "Are you?"

"To be honest, not really. I've known Cruz just as long as I've known you. He's always been protective over you. But lately, he's been extra protective. The dynamic changed when you moved in with each other.

"How can I be so stupid, Mom?"

Mom places her arm around me. "Addison, you're not stupid. People express their feelings in different ways. To someone who lives with their best friend, it's easy to miss these signs."

I choose not to mention tonight and Cruz kissing me in my bed without my consent. Deep down, I know he'd never force himself on me, but it doesn't erase the anger I feel toward him. His advances were uncalled for, and how dare he think I'd easily reciprocate after I walked away from our conversation in confusion.

"Why do men have to be so complicated?"

"They can be just as complicated as women. Look at your father."

"Yeah," I mumble, fidgeting with the gold ring on my finger which my parents gave to me on my twenty-first birthday. "But you and Dad have been together forever. So, it's easy, right?"

Mom purses her lips while thinking. "You always have to work at a marriage or relationship. People evolve, circumstances change, but it should never be hard work. You shouldn't be fighting to stay together. Does that make sense?"

I nod. "But what if being together will hurt someone else?"

"That's a whole other problem."

"But say you're forced to hurt someone you love. Does the guilt ever go away?"

"Yes, no," she says faintly, falling into a digestive silence. "Fate always finds its way. Though, it's not so much guilt but regret. It's easy to look back and think if only I did this or that."

"Like with you and Uncle Julian?" I ask, barely above a whisper in case Dad walks in.

"Julian is where he's meant to be." Mom smiles then rests her hand on top of mine. "But I should have treated him respectfully. Ended things when I knew it wasn't right."

"You mean when Dad walked back into your life and claimed you to be his?"

Mom laughs softly. "Yes, your alpha male of a father was a force to be reckoned with."

"What do you mean was? He still is," I muse.

"Lex Edwards is protective over all the women in his life. It's one of the many reasons why I love him."

I knock into Mom's side playfully. "Look at you, all in love."

"It'll be you one day, Addison."

My smile dissipates at Mom's comments. There's no

more one day. It's too late. I'm in love with a man so unattainable. Correction, attainable if I hurt my best friend.

"Mom..." I begin with, wringing my hands nervously. "There's someone else."

Her chocolate brown eyes light up. "Oh, I see. Do I know the person?"

I nod silently, trying to find the courage to admit the truth. "Yes, you're very acquainted with him."

Moms press their lips together, keeping quiet.

"And this is serious?"

"I don't know. I'm still trying to process it." I lower my gaze then lift my head back to face her. "It's Masen."

Beside me, Mom's lips part, but she tries to hide her surprise. Mom has an excellent poker face given her career choice, so this transient expression is a surprise to me.

"This makes more sense now. You're caught between two brothers," she reiterates, though without judgment. "I understand now why you're trying to process it all."

In front of me sit's three glass jars. Mom is anal about the cookies inside the jar being stacked perfectly. I open one and retrieve a chocolate chip cookie.

"Mom, do you mind if I stay here for a few days? I'm flying to New York for Jessa's dinner. Andy texted me, but I forgot to respond to tell him I'm going. I might fly out early, though, spend an extra day in the city."

Mom places her arm around me, kissing my cheek. It's times like this I miss being here and having her around.

"You never have to ask. This will always be your home."

"But what about Dad?"

"Don't worry about him, okay? I'll take care of him."

I lean into her embrace then bite into my cookie.

"So this whole love thing... worth it?"

Mom squeezes me tighter. "If it's the right man, it's worth every moment. I promise you that."

NINETEEN

MASEN

L ex sits at the head of the table and repeats the numbers projected on the screen in front of us. The data on the graphs is nothing unusual given I have my master's in business and finance.

But today, my attention is elsewhere.

It's Monday morning, two days since Addison walked away from me and chose my brother over us.

Saturday night resulted in me passing out from the bottle of bourbon I drank. That, in turn, equated to the hangover from hell on Sunday morning. It's been a long time since I'd drank that much, but what else was I supposed to do to drown my sorrows?

According to my dad, not fuck another woman.

Sunday was even more challenging. I'd slept until midday, something I never do. I turned off my phone during this time not wanting to be disturbed. In the late afternoon after I'd eaten and gone to the gym, I finally turned it back on. Nothing from Addison, only a blast of messages from Ava.

AVA

> We need to talk

> Are you okay?

> I heard what happened

> Sorry, I didn't hear. I saw.

> Can you please call me? I'm worried about you.

> Both of you, actually.

I ignored the messages, not wanting to talk about it with anyone. The damage is done, so what's there left to say?

And now, I'm here, forced to listen to a man whose daughter is slowly destroying my self-worth.

Across from me, Dad stares brazenly behind his glasses. I focus back onto Lex, counting down the minutes until I can get the hell out of here.

"Thoughts?" Lex asks, taking a seat at the head of the table. "We can execute this in the next few months."

"It's a lot of work," Dad professes, tapping his fingers against the table. "We're up against some big players if we offer print-to-demand facilities."

"You scared, Cooper?" Lex mocks, then glances at me. "Perhaps, I should be looking at the new CEO."

I keep my expression blank, but inside, I'm trying to fight these demons bringing me to a complete standstill.

"The title is yet to be passed on," is all I say.

"I think it's safe to say the title is yours," Lex states with his head held high.

The emerald green in his eyes is too much of a reminder of her. Fuck, I can't even say her goddamn name. I swallow hard, trying to suppress the anger lingering.

"Masen," Mom says in a softer tone. "Everyone in this room agrees that you're the best person for this role. You've worked in this business from the ground up. In the last year, you've almost doubled our profits. Plus, despite me not wanting to admit it, your tough management skills ensure we've gotten rid of the weak and retained only the best."

I lower my eyes, fixating on my hands.

"So, what exactly do you all want from me?"

"Well," Lex begins with, then clears his throat. "Manage the project for the new office building and production facility. I want this up and running within a year which means we need to start moving now."

What Lex is proposing will force me to move away from LA. The distance between here and San Francisco is too much to commute daily. If I agree, then I might as well end things with Addison now.

"I guess I can't say no."

Lex chuckles. "Since when have you ever backed down from hard work?"

"Perhaps, his personal life might have something to do with it," Dad sneers.

My eyes snap in his direction. Is he fucking kidding me right now? And in front of Lex of all people. Sure, fucker, tell your best friend I'm fucking his daughter. Tell him how I owned her inside his house while he sat outside and chilled with his friends.

"Masen?" Mom tilts her head in confusion. "Is there something your father knows that you want to share?"

"Leave the boy alone, you two," Lex chastises. "He's got more important things to worry about than women."

And with that said, I stand up from the table with my shoulders straight and chest out. "Are we done? I have a red-eye to Manhattan tonight."

"Yes, let's reconvene when you're back. I have to head home," he mentions, placing his phone in his suit pocket. "Addison's been staying with us and I'm not sure what's going on. Of course, Charlotte is keeping the details to herself. Woman problems most likely."

I go to open my mouth but then remain tight-lipped. Why would Addison be staying with Lex and Charlie? Something must have happened, and the only person to tell me will be the very person I've tried to avoid all day.

Back inside my office, I dial Ava's number, waiting as it rings out.

"Wait, so you're alive?" she says upon answering.

"Why is Addison staying at your parents'?"

"Addy is at my parents'?"

"Yes, according to your dad."

"Wait, why?"

I press the phone to my forehead, closing my eyes to control my frustration. "I don't know, that's why I'm asking you."

Ava sighs deeply, the sound loud over the speaker. We both fall silent, neither one of us with answers to the question.

"Look, I don't know. Addy isn't one to open up and talk. It might explain why she's gone quiet in the group chat," Ava says in a neutral tone. "Listen, I have to pack for Manhattan and organize the kids. I'll see you at dinner?"

"Is she going?"

"I believe so, but don't get your hopes up, okay?"

"Hopes up?" I repeat in an arctic voice. "She's the one who decided to go home with my brother instead of me. I'm not waiting around like some lovesick fool for her to call me to tell me what, exactly?"

"I know it hurts, but it will work out if you just control your anger, please."

Ava knows me too well, and with her, it's almost impossible to hide the truth.

"I'll see you at dinner, okay?"

"Yeah," is all I mumble before hanging up the phone.

———

The noisy city streets of Manhattan are a welcome change from my chaotic thoughts of late.

I'm standing inside my apartment, dressed in my suit for tonight's dinner. Walking around the living room is my real-tor, Serena. She quietly observes the space, taking notes down as I stand here and wait for her appraisal.

I bought the apartment in college and paid it off over the years after investing in the stock market and pulling out an excellent return. The place is barely used, and word is the property market is predicted to plummet. If I can sell now, I'm able to reinvest elsewhere and get a better return.

"It's a very marketable apartment, Mr. Cooper," Serena compliments with a smile. "Are you sure you want to sell?"

"Yes."

Serena continues to walk around, making her presence known in a very tight white dress. I have to admit, she does have a fantastic body and her ass is...

Don't even look or think about it.

Then, the image of Addison's beautiful face comes to mind. The way she smiled inside my arms as we lay in bed after fucking for hours on end. The memories are like loose shrapnel scattered inside me inflicting pain.

And in an hour's time, I'm forced to face her.

"Listen, Serena. We need to wrap this up," I inform her. "I need to be somewhere in an hour."

There's a knock on the door forcing me to turn around to open it. As soon as it swings open, Addison is standing on the other side, dressed in a bronze-colored silk dress with thin straps. My eyes fall to her chest, gazing at her hard nipples since it's evident there's no bra underneath.

Fuck, I missed her.

And I hate myself for it.

"Addison, what are you doing here?"

As her mouth begins to open, Serena walks toward me. Addison's face falls, then her chin begins to tremble. It takes me a moment to register what's happening, but before I even get a chance to speak, Serena places her hand on my arm.

"I've gotten everything I need. I'll call you later."

Serena leaves the apartment as Addison crosses her arms beneath her chest, pushing her tits up, making her look even sexier. But now isn't the time to focus on that when she's visibly upset and gotten the wrong idea.

"I'm sorry I even came," she mutters beneath her breath.

She attempts to turn around, but I grab her arm tightly.

"Don't," she warns me. "I shouldn't have come here."

"Addison, she's my realtor. I'm listing the apartment and she came to look at it. That's it."

I release my grip but hold her hand instead, leading her into the apartment and closing the door behind us.

"Do you trust me?"

She refuses to look me in the eye but doesn't force my hand away. I have to take it as a good sign, but above anything else, standing this close to her is making me need her even more. The scent of her perfume lingers in the air, and her skin is teasing me with the sexy dress barely covering her body.

"Masen," she breathes, "I don't know what to say about this or Saturday night."

I place my finger on her lips, watching her chest rise and fall. There's time to talk, later. Right now, the primal urge to be inside her is raw and consuming.

"I need you, now..." I grit, cupping her neck and bringing her close to me. "Panties off, I'm going to fuck you quick and hard."

Addison bites down on her lip, a simple move that drives me crazy. Then, she leans down and tugs her laced black panties until they hit the floor between us.

My mouth crashes onto hers with force, tasting her tongue with urgency. I don't wait another minute, lifting her against the door with my hands squeezing her ass.

She fumbles between us to unbutton my suit pants for them to fall. In desperation, she yanks my boxers down, allowing my cock to spring free. Slowly, she eases herself on while gasping. The sensation of her drenched pussy is like ecstasy.

I openly kiss her while thrusting in and out, needing to taste and feel her at the same time. The frenzy within me is building, but I slow down momentarily and take her gaze.

"Give me what I need," I demand of her.

She continues to brave my stare until her hand moves toward the straps of her dress. Teasingly, she pulls them down and exposes her tits. I groan at the sight, biting down on my lip trying to control my urges.

"Good girl, now come for me."

Her hips move in sync with me, the build climbing as I ravage her tits with my mouth, desperate to suck on her perfect pink nipples.

"I'm... I'm..." Addison's words fall short and she throws her head back and moans continuously. The walls of her pussy clench all over me, coercing me to follow as I spurt inside her, along with a grunt.

Our breathing is shallow as we both come down from the high. Carefully, I help her down onto both feet. We quietly fix ourselves up before the silence becomes too loud and words need to be said.

"I think we need to talk," she speaks first. "Can we, please? After dinner."

"Yes," I simply answer, distracted by her lips. "After dinner."

"We should probably go separately if that's okay?"

"Fine by me."

She reaches out for the doorknob then opens the door. "I'll see you later."

Before she closes it, I call her name prompting her to turn around. With a longing stare, she waits for me to speak.

"Addison, you look beautiful tonight."

She nods, then follows with a grin. "You look pretty damn handsome yourself, Mr. Cooper."

"And one more thing..."

I take a step toward her, cupping her chin to plant a kiss on her lips. As we pull apart, she expels a soft moan.

"Just like in the book," she whispers.

Then, she turns around toward the elevator, saying good-bye, just for now.

Catching up with the Edwards girls and their cousins is always chaotic. Throw Eric into the mix and it's a circus.

There are a lot of wine and cocktails for the girls—plus harder stuff for men who don't drink candy-flavored shit.

The food keeps coming, as does the laughter. Eric is non-stop, as usual, but everyone is enjoying themselves. I try my best to involve myself yet sitting across from Addison makes it difficult. Aside from her teasing me in the silk dress she wears, Ava is watching the both of us making it challenging to act normal.

However, this night is all about Jessa. We toast to her and her success, especially since her book is making our company a hell of a lot of money.

I'm happy for Andy and Jessa, given how hard it was for

them to get together finally. According to Andy, Jessa's split from her husband wasn't easy since she has a son.

Nash, Addison's cousin, is sitting beside me. We talk for most of the night about sports, and his trip to Miami. The guy likes his women, not shy to admit his conquests. He reminds me of a young Rocky.

There are a few stolen glances throughout the night with Addison, but I catch Jessa watching us at one time. It's not long before this all comes out, and everyone will know.

But for now, Addison and I need privacy to work out what's going on between us since I'm struggling to understand myself.

Andy leans in, turning his head to keep his voice low. "We're going to head out now."

I pat his shoulder. "Good luck, brother."

As they say goodbye to everyone, the rest of us remain behind until Nash calls boredom.

"Ava, can we get into your dad's club?"

"Which one?" she questions, resting her head on Austin.

"After Dark."

"We can make it happen," Will says, prompting us to all stand up.

I'd been to Lex's club before, knowing it's just two blocks over. Nash is walking along with me as Addison is holding hands with Eric. The guy hasn't stopped talking all night long.

"I was once involved in a certain situation at the After Dark."

"If this is sexual, I don't want to know," Addison complains.

"It involves Lex and Charlie. The kitchen. And fingering—"

Addison slaps his arm. "What's wrong with you?"

"What?" Eric drags. "It was hot."

"Maybe, to you. I don't need to know these details."

Nash pulls his phone out, having received a text. He types back quickly, then tucks his phone back into his pocket.

"Just got a message from Cruz. He's coming to After Dark."

Addison stops mid-step. "He's here? In Manhattan?"

"Yeah, but he couldn't make dinner since he had an important meeting today and had to catch a later flight," Nash informs her. "You didn't know?"

I'm drawn to how her shoulders tense, and how she avoids my persistent stare. Something isn't right, but I have no clue what it is or what happened. If Addison has been staying at her parents' house, I'm assuming she got into a fight with Cruz.

A big one for her to make such a drastic move.

The curiosity begins to eat away at me. There's no chance to pull her aside and ask because we arrive at the club.

Will speaks to the security team, who let us all in. Inside, it's your typical club scene—dark with neon lights and loud music. There's a VIP area upstairs that Will has organized for us during the short walk here.

We get ourselves settled inside the gold booth, waiting for the servers to bring us drinks. Most of us order the same drinks, and notably, Addison barely takes a sip from hers. She's unusually quiet, but once again, I'm unable to pull her aside to talk.

"Let's do shots," Nash announces.

"Shots?" Amelia complains. "I'm breastfeeding."

"Me too," Ava says.

"Did you guys have to be so gross?" Nash scowls.

"Gross?" The girls repeat in a high-pitched tone.

Will hides his smirk behind his glass. "You're in trouble now, boy."

Nash is saved by Cruz's arrival. He greets everyone with

hugs, stopping when his eyes fall upon Addison. She stands up, but her body language is far from accommodating. The embrace is quick, the two of them pulling apart swiftly.

I glance in Ava's direction as she shrugs. My instincts warn me something has happened and judging by the way they're interacting, it's not something good.

And can possibly destroy me.

My mind begins to wander to a dark place, despite the vibrant energy inside the club. Everyone is busy chatting over the noise, yet the stiff air makes it difficult for me to breathe. I lean over to Nash to tell him I'm going downstairs.

There's a lot of people here tonight, bunching up in small crowds. I walk in solitude without looking at anyone else, displaying a hard expression to avoid the female attention making eyes at me. When I reach the bar, I order a double shot of whisky straight away.

The liquor goes down nicely, so I order another, but then a familiar hand reaches out in front of me and takes my drink.

Cruz drinks it without even asking, slamming it on the counter to order another.

"That was my drink, in case it didn't register."

"I need it more," he replies in an agitated tone.

This is my chance to find out what the hell is going on. I highly doubt he knows anything is happening between Addison and me since he's standing here next to me.

Resting my elbows on the counter, I take the next drink served but nurse it instead.

"So, upstairs, Addison didn't look too pleased to see you."

He lets out a long-winded sigh. "She's probably not."

"Did something happen between you two?"

Cruz doesn't respond straight away, drinking the whisky in one go and ordering another. The bartender warns him to slow down, to which Cruz argues back that he'll get the fucker fired.

"This needs to stay between us..." he warns me. My jaw clenches, not liking the sound of this. "Coach thinks I've got a high chance of being drafted to an NFL team."

I draw back, surprised it's not what I think. "You've worked hard. So, I'm not understanding the problem?"

"I told Addison I don't want to leave because..." he trails off, then strains, "... I told her I'm in love with her."

My brother's admission hit's me like a thousand daggers to the chest. Here he is, professing his love to her. I don't even have the courage to admit how I feel despite how much we've fucked over the last few weeks.

I'm unsure what to say, but then it comes to mind.

"What did Addison say?"

"She freaked out, of course. I mean, it fucking hurt you know. I thought there was something between us despite her being distant of late," Cruz admits with a tightened voice. "But there's more. Something I'm not proud of ..."

The pounding inside my ears isn't from the loud music, but the beat of my heart. My rushed breathing causes my throat to dry out at the same time my hands clench, and unclench, waiting for the storm to hit.

"What happened?" I grit through my teeth.

"She was sleeping, and I..."

"You what?"

"I went to her bedroom," he continues with a shaky voice. "I'm not proud, okay? I'd been drinking and—"

"What did you do?"

"I forced myself on her," he sputters, then rushes. "It was just a kiss, but I should have listened when she tried to tell me to stop."

Beneath my clothing, a rush of heat spreads all over my skin. The adrenaline runs through my veins as my lips pull back baring my teeth.

Slowly, my hand moves toward my chest with my fist

clenched. As my nostrils flare, I swiftly turn around to face the man who inflicted all this rage and pain.

"Why are you looking at me like that?" Cruz questions, pulling back. "I said it was a mistake and I'm not proud of what I—"

My fist connects with his face before he finishes his sentence. The pain ricochets through my hand, causing me to clench tighter. There's a commotion around us as Cruz tries to retaliate, managing to swipe the corner of my jaw.

His bloodied face is staring at me, ready to strike again until arms pull me back. They belong to Will as Austin holds back Cruz.

Addison runs toward us, standing in the middle. Her pained eyes dart back and forth, then they fixate only on me.

"Addison, don't."

"We're over," she threatens in a cold voice. "I never want to see you again."

"This is my fault?" I argue back, my blood pumping like an animal defending his kingdom from the wild. "You keep fucking choosing him! I was never your first choice. I was convenient for sex and that's it."

"Yeah," she grits with a cold stare. "And without sex, we're nothing. Goodbye, Masen."

And just like that, our fate is sealed.

My brother won, just like I predicted all along.

TWENTY

ADDISON

My head rests against the pillow as tears silently stream down my cheeks.

A painful tightness inside my throat makes it difficult to breathe, but what's the point of breathing air to survive.

I'm left without two people I love.

The moment I saw Cruz tonight, I knew it would be awkward between us. I was just hoping we'd be able to talk in private. Being away for a few days gave me time to think and calm down. The truth is, I don't want to give up on our friendship over one mistake, or albeit, poor judgment from him.

We'd spent a lifetime building a friendship other people envied. Our time together is a part of who I am. This isn't the type of friendship you can toss to the side and ghost.

But I also can't give him what he wants.

I'm in love with Masen.

And my bleeding heart is singing the saddest of tunes while crying a river of tears over a man who hurt my best friend.

I didn't stay a single minute longer, escaping the scene because the sobs inside my chest were raw and ready to burst out into the open for everyone to see. My parents' penthouse was too far to walk, so I cabbed it for what felt like the longest ten minutes of my life. It didn't help that the music playing on the radio was "Yellow" by Coldplay.

One of my favorite songs.

As I sat there, memorizing each lyric in my head, the song took a whole other meaning. It hurt, all over, each lyric, and every beat. I begged myself not to cry, holding it in until the door to my parents' place closed behind me.

The loneliness inside this big room is loud and brutal. But then, I hear the quiet footsteps I've known my whole life. The bed moves from my sisters lying on each side of me.

Holding back my tears is challenging as I now lay on my back, staring at the ceiling. My nose, which was running, is now clogging up and making it hard to breathe.

"It hurts," Millie whispers, holding onto my hand. "Love is so powerful that when you finally find it, its absence leaves the darkest hole inside your heart."

"What did I do wrong?"

"Addy, we all make mistakes. But sometimes those mistakes lead to bigger things, you know."

"Ava is right. If Will didn't come to the Hamptons, I'd never have screwed him against Dad's car and betrayed Austin. That moment defined us."

"And if that moment didn't happen, I would never have slept with Austin after a drunk New Year's Eve, and there would be no Emmy or River."

We lay in silence while I think about fate and my sisters. I'm nothing like them, coming to the realization that they're screwed up despite where they ended up. The thought makes my tears stop, wondering why I've never truly figured this out until now.

"The both of you are messed up," I tell them honestly. "How am I even related to you?"

"Well," Ava begins. "Once upon a time, Daddy shot his load into Mommy, who said she was on birth control but forgot to take it. The end."

The three of us laugh together, a small moment which feels nice. Our laughter follows with a long-united sigh which, in turn, makes us laugh again.

"According to Alexa, the way you were doing it in the cellar will not get you knocked up again," Millie snickers.

"Hang on. How much did she watch?" Ava groans.

"Enough to know you don't get pregnant catching the chocolate train," Millie teases.

I manage another smile. "Oh, Eric..."

"Look, I enjoy it, okay? Don't judge me."

Millie shrugs. "Will enjoys it when my breasts accidentally leak when I'm riding him."

I almost choke on my saliva. "What? Oh God, I'll never look at him the same."

"It must be a guy thing. Austin enjoys it too."

"Um, you guys are weird, and this conversation is weird."

Ava huffs. "Knowing that Masen is a former playboy, I'm sure he has his preferences in the bedroom too."

"Yeah," I mumble, remembering tonight before dinner. My immediate assumption of the woman at his apartment was that he was sleeping with her. Boy, was I wrong. Another fuck-up on my end. "Or bathroom at Mom and Dad's place, his office, parking garage ..."

A hand smacks my arm, causing me to scowl. "Ava, that hurt!"

"I'm just so excited you unleashed your dirty side. Masen is like a brother, so don't give me any more details but his office? That's hot."

"I fucked Will once in his office..." Millie trails off, then continues. "... while Dad called."

Ava and I gasp at the same time.

"Poor Dad." Ava giggles.

"Poor Dad?" Millie repeats. "The man is notorious for screwing our mother whenever and wherever. Why is his sex drive not slowing down? No wonder Alexa is desperate to move out."

"So basically, we're genetically made up of two dirty people, and therefore it's in our blood to get our kink on," I say.

"You said it, sister," Ava quips.

I take a deep breath, but then tonight comes back like a nightmare, unwilling to fade away into the night.

"You guys, what am I going to do?"

Millie sighs heavily. "You allow yourself to feel the pain. It'll hurt, make you feel like you can't breathe, and then you'll wake up one day and know exactly what you're going to do."

"Are you sure?"

"It might be tomorrow, the day after, next week, or next month. There's no time on mending a broken heart," Millie says faintly. "But that moment will hit when you know you can't live without them."

My sisters don't leave my side for the rest of the night. I count my blessings, and two of them are holding onto me for dear life. I'm not sure what I'd do without them, realizing the importance of family when your darkest hour has finally struck.

Millie was right. I felt all the emotions she said I would and more. I stayed in Manhattan for a few days, distracting myself with Millie and Ava's children. There's nothing like a trip to the zoo with three kids and two crying babies. The number of times we stopped for feeding and diaper changes was next level.

I do everything possible not to think about Masen, but the pain refuses to subside. As days pass, my mistakes shine brighter in the light. He's not to blame entirely, and I'm far from perfect. Love has made me do crazy things. If this is love, I understand everything Mom said. The question is, am I fighting for us to stay together, and will this fight be a lifetime of heartache or the start to a new beginning?

Back in LA, I continue to stay at Mom and Dad's before confronting Cruz again. His actions in all of this aren't innocent, but I recognize his pain too. I just don't know how to approach him right now, barely able to hold myself together.

It's another late night with insomnia welcoming me to the dark side. Wearing my slippers and robe, I shuffle to the kitchen to find Mom and Dad laughing quietly. I still my movements, watching how Dad gazes at her lovingly as she tells a story. Before entering, I clear my throat.

"Addison, come sit with us," Mom offers.

"I'm not interrupting, am I?"

Dad motions for me to sit beside them. "It's been nice having you back. Though I don't know the full extent to why you're back."

As I sit down, my eyes fall to my hands resting on the table. "It's complicated."

"Does the complication have anything to do with the incident at After Dark?"

It's impossible to hide anything from this man, but unlike my sisters, I'm not scared of his reaction. Dad is Dad in my eyes. He'll have an opinion, but I know he'll never stop loving me.

"Yes," I answer, then intake a deep breath. "I've always promised myself that when the time came, I'd think rationally and not allow my life to be dictated by raw emotions. Yet, here we are =..."

"Addison," Dad calls softly. "You've always been a strong-willed woman, and I'll always be proud of the person you've become. But what you're going through right now, it's a part of life. Pulling through this and determining what to fight for, it'll make you stronger in the end."

I bow my head. "I love him, Dad. I was never supposed to fall in love with Masen, of all people."

"Fate, honey. Always in the stars," Mom says with a smile.

"Well, the stars hate me right now. I've hurt him, he's hurt me. We've both hurt Cruz. I don't know the answer to any of this."

"Just like your sisters, they pulled through the hard times and look at them now," Dad reminds me.

A small laugh escapes me. "Dad, you were their hard time."

Dad nods with agrement. "Hmmm, so I'm the common problem, is that what you're saying?"

I lean in and rest my head on his arm like I've done a million times before. "Not once did I worry about you, if I'm being honest."

"That's because you're a grown woman, making adult decisions. Unlike your sisters, boys and men were the least on your priority list. So, this is your time. I'll make peace with that. Amelia broke me entirely, Ava has aged me from the minute she hit puberty." Dad kisses the top of my head then strokes my cheek. "But you, my beautiful Addison, have been a father's blessing to raise."

With a lonesome tear falling down my cheek, I gaze at the man who has just given me the ultimate praise.

"I don't know what to say," I choke.

Mom pats my hand with a soft chuckle. "You take that compliment from the great Lex Edwards."

I smile at both of them, wondering how I got so blessed to call these two people my parents.

"Thank you," I finally say, then take a breath with a knowing smile. "I think I know what my next step is."

"Good morning, Dr. Jenner."

Dr. Jenner glances up with a welcoming smile. Her burgundy-colored hair is tied up into a tight bun today, unlike every other time when it's usually out.

"Good morning, Addison. How was your week and trip to Manhattan?"

I purse my lips into a hard smile. "Eventful."

She nods knowingly. "I see. Perhaps your day may pick up?"

"Is there anything you need me to do this morning?"

Dr. Jenner places her notepad down on the reception desk, focusing her attention on me. I assume she's about to give me important instructions, wishing I'd grabbed my notebook out to not look like an incompetent idiot.

"There's a patient of mine waiting in room two. Would you mind keeping them company while I just get a few things done?"

"Of course, Dr. Jenner."

I place my bag down but hold onto my coffee since I've barely gotten any sleep. Trying to get dressed this morning proved challenging. I had nothing to wear, so I raided Mom's closet. Stupid me should've knocked since Dad and Mom came out of the bathroom wearing only towels. I mean, why do they have to hang in there together?

Oh God, I think I need therapy to erase the awkward moment.

A simple gray tunic dress with a thin black belt is what I settled for. I paired it with the classic black Louboutins Mom bought me when I got this job.

I knock on the door, then enter slowly with a smile, only to stop mid-step at the sight of Cruz sitting on the couch.

"What the hell are you doing here?" I question in shock.

Cruz stands up. "We need to talk, Addy."

My arms fold beneath my chest with a struggle since I'm trying to still hold onto my coffee. "You can't come into my place of work and demand to talk to me about a personal matter."

"I know, but I need you to listen to me, please."

"You have two minutes," I point."And I better not lose my job."

Cruz raises his hands in defeat. "Addy, I need to apologize. What I did to you was uncalled for. I'm ashamed to have put you in a position where you didn't feel safe with me."

I bow my head, taking a deep breath.

"I'm not perfect, and I've spent most of my adult life relying on you for support. I do love you. I always have and always will," he says, then pauses. "But I need to learn how to live my life without you as my life jacket."

We both fall quiet with so much to say. The shift in our relationship was always going to happen. I just didn't expect it to happen this soon.

"I'm sorry I lied to you about Masen."

He nods, pressing his lips together to keep his mouth shut.

"I've hurt you, and I own that mistake," I continue, willing the guilt to ease with my admission. "I just wasn't thinking."

Cruz shuffles his footsteps while glancing at the floor.

"He's hurting, you know," is all he says.

"You've spoken to him?"

"Spoken," he confirms with a straight face. "And seen him."

"I... I don't know what to say."

Cruz takes two steps to be closer to where I stand. "I have to go. My flight leaves in two hours."

"Flight?"

He grins proudly. "Yeah, it's time to show the big guys what I got."

"When are you back?"

"Two days," he informs me. "Why, you gonna miss me?"

I put my coffee down and extend my arms to invite his embrace. The smell of his cologne is nostalgic and reminds me of all the good times we've had as best friends. We can't go back to our careless days, but I'm glad we made the memories that will last forever.

"You'll call me every five minutes, right?"

He moves a stray hair away from my face. "Yeah, you can't get rid of me that easily. But, Addy, promise me something?"

My feet take a step back with a smile still on my face. "Anything for you."

"Go to him," he urges with an upturned face. "Life is too short to sit around and wait for fate to intervene. You love him, then tell him."

"But what if he doesn't feel the same way?"

"I bet on all the stars in the universe, you're proven wrong."

TWENTY-ONE

MASEN

There was no chance I was going to stay in Manhattan a minute longer.

A private plane flew me back home, where I stayed locked up with bottles of whisky, bourbon, and anything spare left in my liquor cabinet. A quick email telling my parents I'm working from home got them off my back.

The pain came in waves—anger, resentment, and grief— three very different emotions are wreaking havoc on my fragile ego.

Addison's voice replays in my head like a broken record, unable to play anything else.

"We're over."

My jaw is still bruised from my brother's retaliation, but the pain is nothing compared to the emptiness of Addison gone from my life.

So, I do what's necessary for such circumstances. I begin packing my things ready for my move to San Francisco.

The tedious task is mind-numbing and coupled with the lack of sleep and dark circles around my eyes, it's better than being in the office and having to deal with people.

It's late-night when there's a knock on my door. I half-expect it to be Mom or Ava—knowing those women are over-bearing with the need to wrap me in cotton wool like I'm a goddamn baby.

Before I open the door, I inhale a breath then finally open it. My brother is standing on the other side with a slightly bruised nose, wearing his favorite jersey and a bottle of whisky in his hand.

"You look like shit," he tells me.

"So do you," I counter while turning my back and walking away from him. "Why are you here?"

"Waiting for my apology."

I fold my arms beneath my chest. "You'll be waiting a long time. It's easier if you see yourself out.

Cruz ignores me, walking toward the kitchen and retrieving two glasses from the cupboard. He pours the whisky, leaving out the ice, then walks over and hands it to me.

"Drink," he commands.

I drink it because it'll temporarily numb the pain, not from his command.

Cruz scans the apartment, eyeing all the boxes stacked. "You're moving?"

The warm liquor hits the back of my throat, but I continue to drink until the glass is empty. "Yes."

"Do Mom and Dad know?"

"It's their idea."

"Where are you moving to?"

"San Francisco," I answer flatly.

"I'm not going to apologize to you for punching your face. You deserved it after hitting mine. You won't get an apology from me because I've done nothing wrong to you," he states with confidence. "Addison is the person who deserves an apology. What I did to her was wrong. I crossed the boundary, and I hate myself for it."

"I won't argue that," I mutter.

"Don't do this to her."

My head snaps as I glance at him with contempt. "I'm not good enough for her. So, before you want to place blame on me, I've done nothing wrong but fallen for a girl who doesn't feel the same way."

It pains me to even admit the truth to someone else, especially since I haven't even accepted the truth myself.

"You're a dick," he shouts. "She fucking loves you. If you can stop acting like a self-entitled jerk, show her you fucking love her."

I swallow the lump inside my throat, shutting my eyes with no strength to fight at this moment.

"She made her intentions clear," I say in a low voice.

"Yeah, because she's pissed you hurt me. She loves both of us for different reasons. We're the reason why she's hurting now. I don't want to hurt her anymore. I love her and always will. It's why I'm going to try my best to get picked, then move on with my career."

I hate the truth to his words. My anger displayed at the club resulted in me punching his face, knowing Addison disapproves of such violence. She studies psych, and how I reacted goes against everything she believes in.

So, I swallow my pride.

"I'm sorry I hit you."

"Eh, it was a pretty pussy punch."

The corner of my mouth curves up slightly. "Same goes for you, brother."

We both sit on the leather couch to pour the remnants in the bottle. It doesn't take us long to finish between the two of us.

"How do you feel about trying out for the big guns?" I ask, knowing how important this is to him.

"Ready, nervous, I dunno," he responds while shrugging. "I've waited my whole life for this.

"Show them the real you. That's all there is to this."

"Yeah, you're right. I just gotta be confident, like you," Cruz professes but pauses briefly. "I know we don't exactly get along, but for what it's worth, I've always looked up to you."

I cock my head in confusion. "Me?"

"Yeah, I mean Dad and Mom are proud as fuck over you. You're destined to be the next Lex Edwards."

A small chuckle escapes me. "C'mon, no one competes with him."

"Will does."

"Eh, he thinks he does, but Lex is the king of the throne."

Cruz laughs. "Yeah, I guess."

"But listen," I continue, placing my hand on his shoulder. "You can do this, okay? If you think Mom and Dad are proud of me? They're equally proud of you."

"You really think so?"

I squeeze my baby brother's shoulder. "I know so."

The receptionist leads me down the long corridor toward Lex's office.

His new building is quite an architectural eyesore. Glass windows everywhere with panoramic views of LA.

She knocks on the door then opens it. Lex is sitting behind his desk on the phone.

"Gordon, I need to call you back."

He hangs up the phone to stand up, extending his hand to shake mine. I do so to be courteous but remain standing rather than sitting down.

"Please, sit."

"I'll continue to stand if you don't mind."

"If that's what you prefer," he simply says.

My hands move inside the pockets of my navy pants. I begin to pace the area in front of his desk, followed by nervously removing my left hand to run through my hair.

Then, I stop and stare directly into Lex's eyes.

"I love Addison," I exclaim, straightening my shoulders to muster any confidence to continue. "I'm telling you because I don't want you to issue me an ultimatum. I will work hard to uphold the position you've granted me as CEO, but not at the expense of being forced to give up the one woman I love."

"Masen, I—"

"I know, Lex, your daughters are your world," I continue, running on adrenaline for finally admitting the truth. "I'd never intentionally hurt Addison. But I love her, and I know you haven't been easy on the men who have walked into your girls' lives."

Lex's still expression doesn't waver, then he raises his brows. "Are you finished now?"

I let out a breath. "Yes."

"I'll admit my actions with Will were uncalled for. I was scared of losing my firstborn to a man I felt used me at the time for his own pleasure," he admits, catching me by surprise. "However, Addison is not Amelia. Nor is she Ava. She will do the right thing, as will you."

"So that means ..."

"It means, I will stay out of your relationship. I trust you both to make decisions right for both of you. Regarding your new role, you were, and always will be, the right man to lead the company."

It's the greatest of compliments from the king.

"Thank you," I manage, lost for words.

"Now, don't you have somewhere you need to be? My daughter is patient, but fate isn't, my son."

The black Mercedes pulls into the parking garage, stopping beside me. I exit the car at the same time as Mom and Dad. They're both still dressed in work clothes, despite having to leave for a flight to San Francisco in an hour.

"Masen," Mom murmurs, reaching to caress my cheek with the back of my hand. "Why didn't you tell me?"

I shrug, unable to explain how my emotions were all over the place, and falling in love hurt more than it should have.

"Because, Presley, he's an arrogant jerk," Dad concedes.

A smirk plays on my lips. "Like father, like son, huh?"

Dad simpers then reaches out to pull me in for a fatherly embrace. Mom bows her head, trying to control her tears. What's with women crying all the time?

"And look how blessed I've been to have two talented sons and one very beautiful wife who puts up with all my shit."

I place my hand on his shoulder. "And to think, all because you couldn't keep your pierced dick in your pants. You just had to infuriate your co-worker."

Dad chuckles as Mom shakes her head in shame, then says, "Masen, one spontaneous night led to your existence."

"Should have pulled out big fella, save you the stress," I tease.

"I did," Dad sneers, only for Mom's mouth to fall open from his admission. "But one of those slippery little suckers got in early."

"Okay," Mom interrupts with a huff, handing me the silver key. "What you called us for."

I take the key from her hand, staring at it with thought.

"You can do this, Masen," she coerces in a soft voice. "Some things were always in the stars."

My arms reach to hug her, allowing her a moment to hug

me overbearingly as mothers do. When we pull away, my parents get back in the car.

"Good luck," they say in unison.

"No luck needed," I respond with a grin. "Fate, right?"

"See you soon, son."

Dad drives off, leaving me standing here alone. I exhale a loud breath and then take the stairs to the apartment. The key takes a few jiggles to unlock the door, but once I'm inside the apartment, I smell her scent everywhere. It's like the morphine to my pain, calming my nerves to allow me to sit down and wait.

And wait is what I do.

But not for long.

The doorknob rattles, causing my stomach to flip in nerves. *What if she tells me it's still over and is unable to forgive me for hurting Cruz?* My shoulders drag low with shallow yet audible breaths leaving my chest.

Fuck! This is it.

The door opens wide, followed by Addison removing her keys then glancing up. She jumps on the spot, clutching her chest in shock.

"Oh my god," she chokes, becoming speechless. "What are you doing here?"

I stand up, finally straightening my shoulders while she closes the door behind her. My eyes are drawn to the curves of her body in the dress she wears down to the heels on her feet.

Concentrate.

Slowly, she turns around, looking more beautiful than ever.

"I'm here to apologize to you for the hurt I caused. I never intended to put you in the middle of you and your best friend. I was angry Cruz did that to you, and it was the only way at the time I knew how to react."

Addison places her purse down, placing her hands on her hips with a pinched mouth.

"Don't you think you should be apologizing to your brother?"

"I have."

"Wait, he didn't say anything," she responds in confusion.

"Perhaps he felt the matter needed to stay between us brothers."

Addison's mouth falls open. I knew the comment would goad a reaction from her. I'm just waiting for her explosion to come any time now.

"Oh, so never mind, I've been his best friend his entire life," she bites with frustration. Now, it's all about bro code?"

"You look hot when you're angry," I tease.

She shakes her head then rips her gaze away to the floor. "That's neither here nor there."

I take steps to bring me closer to her. Then, I reach out and lift her chin so our eyes meet.

"I love you, Addison. I'm terrified of how deeply in love I am with you. But I know my life is nothing unless you're in it."

A gentle sigh parts from Addison's lips. "Masen, I said things out of anger. The emotions were raw. I was in over my head trying to balance a relationship I thought was forbidden, but only in my eyes. I never gave us a chance, scared of what others may think. But in the end, what matters is us. I love you too, and I'm terrified just as much."

My hands cup her face, bringing her in for a soft kiss. The taste of her warm lips spreads to every inch of my body, allowing me the peace my soul deserves. Addison loves me, and in the end, that's all I'll ever need.

"I'm sorry," she whispers with a single tear falling down her cheek.

I wipe it away with my thumb then beg her to look at me.

"We're done with the sneaking around. I'm ready for us to begin our lives with one another. This is it, Addison. I love you, and if we do this, it's for life."

She places her hands flat on my chest with a grin. "You might want to talk to the old fella. Run that by him before you steal his favorite daughter."

"I'll tell Ava you said that," I tease.

"Don't you dare!"

"And by the way, been there, done that."

"Wait... what do you mean?"

"Lex is a good man. That's all."

"You can't just say Lex is a good man, and that's all," she complains. "You're a jerk."

"Yeah." I grin, teasing her lips again with my mouth. "But I'm your jerk now."

The alarm on my phone alerts me of the time. I pull it out of my pocket, knowing I have to leave in the next few minutes.

"What's wrong?"

"I have to leave."

"Leave? But what about all the make-up sex we're supposed to have. In this book I read recently, the make-up sex was off the charts. The woman came three times in a row."

I cock my head with a playful smirk. "I thought you didn't read romance?"

"It's for research purposes," she admits, trying to hide her smile. "But really, you have to go?"

"I have a plane to catch to San Francisco."

"Why San Francisco?"

I drop my hand to hers with ease, then raise her hand to my lips to plant a soft kiss. "You see, my brother has an important meeting, and he needs all the support he can get."

Addison's eyes widen. "You're going to watch Cruz try out?"

I nod, keeping my smile fixed.

"Is there any room on the plane for me?" she asks, hopeful.

With a dismissive glance, I rub my chin. "Hmm, it is a private plane, so the only room for you is on my lap."

A beautiful smile spreads across my girls face. I take a moment to thank my lucky stars. She's all mine, and then, our future in front of us flashes like a shooting star in the night—marriage, family—a whole life together which begins today.

"It's going to be quite some ride," she whispers with a grin.

"You up for it?"

"With you?" Addison murmurs, running her finger across my bottom lip. "I'll ride with you for life."

EPILOGUE

ADDISON

Three Months Later

"Hurry up. We're going to be late."

Inside the bathroom, I finish brushing my hair then choose to place it in a ponytail. Living with a man is exhausting at times. It's been two months since I moved to San Francisco, a month after Masen. Fortunately, Dr. Jenner owned a second practice, and I was able to transfer here. My schooling required a bit more juggling, but I managed to make it work as well.

I step outside in my red-lace bra and panties when I look somewhat presentable. Masen's annoyed face quickly morphs into a lustful stare as he looks me up and down.

"Okay, now we're going to be really late," he complains, taking steps closer to me, then grabbing my ass and burying his head into my chest. "I'll be one minute."

I push him away, shaking my head. "Nope, you're a stickler for time, and if we factor in traffic, we'll miss the start."

Masen throws his hands to his face, letting out a groan.

While he's cussing, I place the matching jersey on but scour the bedroom for my jeans.

"Now, you're being a tease in the jersey and panties. C'mon, Addison, how about just a blow job?"

My lips press flat. "Because that's not selfish at all."

Finally, I see my jeans folded in the cupboard. I grab the pair, attempting to shimmy my way into them, followed by placing on my white high-top sneakers.

"Fine, I'll make a deal with you," he says in a serious tone.

"Oh yeah, go ahead, state your deal."

"The team wins. I get whatever I want."

"That's so broad," I drag out while rolling my eyes. "Be specific."

Masen stands in front of me then slides his thumb inside my mouth. I react almost instantly, but I try to remain unaffected.

"I get to finally fuck this pretty little asshole of yours tonight," he teases.

I step back in panic. "Whoa, cowboy. We talked about this. You know, how you have a big cock plus a piercing."

"We did talk, but you didn't listen. Once you try it, I promise you'll beg for more."

An obnoxious laugh leaves my mouth. "I promise you I won't beg. I'd bet my whole life I won't make it past the tip of your cock going in."

"Hmm, is that so?"

"Yes."

"So, it's a deal?"

I cross my arms but look away. "Fine. But you get the tip, and that's it. Now, let's go before we're late."

The crowd is cheering loudly in the stands.

We're packed in like sardines which isn't unusual, bumping shoulders at the edge of our seats as the scoreboard continues its countdown. There's more nervous energy amongst us, several fans closing their eyes and mumbling some sort of prayer to the polar opposite—profanities being yelled against the already loud noises coming from the stadium speakers.

Masen is the worst offender of all. He'd put a sailor to shame with the words he's yelled out.

Cruz's team is killing it. My eyes wander to where Cruz is standing with a serious expression.

Sixty seconds are left on the clock, each number drawing down with the pressure mounting. The beat of my heart is drumming so loud, ready to burst through an oversized matching jersey Masen bought for him and me.

C'mon guys. You can do this.

The buzzer finally rings loudly. The supporters jumps to cheer the team's victory win.

"YES!"

I fist pump the air, screaming at the top of my lungs until I fall into a fit of coughs from my dry throat. My arms unknowingly throw themselves over the girl beside me, hugging her tight while we continue to holler proudly. Then, I turn to face Masen as he watches his brother proudly.

Abandoning our chairs, we run down the steps with excitement. We stop at the fence, then wait for Cruz. He turns around, a smile filled with pride as he runs over. Masen embraces him with a congratulatory pat on the back. Then, Cruz turns to me, and I hug his sweaty body fiercely.

"Can you believe it, guys? We fucking won!"

"You totally killed it, bro," Masen cheers, then leans in. "By the way, the redhead is waiting for you. Damn ..."

I smack Masen on the arm. "Finish that sentence, and you die."

"Aw, Addy is jealous," Cruz teases. "Okay, listen. I'm not coming over tonight because, well, my dick is more important."

My face scrunches at his vulgarity.

"But, tomorrow, we're on, yeah?"

"Just us," I tell him. "Masen is flying to Manhattan with my dad."

"So, Indian?"

"Fine, but this time, make sure you bring your own toilet paper since you wiped us clean last time."

Cruz brings his hand to his forehead to salute me. "Yes, mother."

The redhead makes eyes with him, prompting him to leave us to join her. Masen grabs my hand as we walk back up the stairs and to the parking lot. When we get inside the car, it's a traffic jam to even get out. It makes the ten-minute drive home feel like nothing.

Back inside the apartment, Masen wraps his arms around my waist.

"So, they won. Now you owe me."

I follow with a nervous laugh. "About that ..."

He doesn't stop to listen, pushing me toward the bedroom. My back is still facing him, but slowly, he begins to strip off all my clothes, leaving me in only my panties.

"A deal is a deal," he whispers in my ear. "Panties down, now."

His controlling tone ignites the flame inside of me, and by demand, I drop my panties to the floor.

"Good girl. Now, on all fours, I'm hungry."

My hands fall flat onto the bed with my knees in position. His soft breath lingers behind me, causing my body to shiver in delight. Teasingly, he kisses in between my thighs before I demand he eat me out like the hungry beast he is.

I'm barely able to control the orgasm as his tongue flicks

my clit, combined with his fingers sliding in and out. Just as I'm about to fall into a blissful finish, he stops entirely.

"Wh ... why did you stop?" I ask, out of breath.

"Relax," he murmurs, rubbing the tip of his cock against my ass. "We don't even need any lube. You're wet enough."

The thought of it going in my ass terrifies me. Before the panic sets in, I bring my fingers to my pussy, rubbing it slowly to distract myself.

"Perfect, play with yourself while I enter you."

The tip begins to move in as I wince in pain, shutting my eyes. He completely stops, rubbing my back, then continues to inch his way in again. The pain starts, but then it subsides when he's entirely in.

"Are you okay?" he asks softly.

I nod.

"I promise to go slow."

He begins to move at an unhurried pace, slow enough for my body to adjust and the sensation to build. His hands grip onto my hips tightly as an unexplainable fullness reaches my core. In a matter of seconds, my skin is covered in goosebumps, and every thrust is pushing me closer to climax.

I throw my head back with a moan, pushing my ass deeper into him.

"Beg me for it," he demands.

"Fuck me harder," I strain, slamming into him harder. "Fuck my ass harder, please."

And just like that, his groan is enough to send my body into a beautiful abyss of an orgasm, and the ripples of pleasure last several seconds longer than usual.

Our heavy breaths echo in the room, but before he pulls himself out, he leans over to kiss my shoulder.

"I love you." He hums.

My hand reaches around, pulling him back into me. "I love you even more, Mr. Cooper."

And that's how fate played its part. It brought our families together through the bond of children. Then, in turn, we've created a bond of our own.

Falling in love with Masen Cooper was never part of my plan, but fate always finds its way into our lives.

It may have taken a couple of tries, but in the end, we're both where we're supposed to be.

And we found our fate on the road we'd both been avoiding.

Love.

THE END

COMING UP NEXT...

Craving Love: An Age Gap Romance
The Secret Love Series Book 1

I'm done playing by my father's rules.
Lex Edwards may rule the business world, but he no longer
controls me.

We did, however, come to one agreement—I'm allowed to
take a gap year before college to travel through Europe. But,
one year to the day, I must return home.

On my travels, I met April. She's like me, escaping her family
life back home. April offers me a place to stay. I'll take
anything over going back home to my controlling father.

That's when I am offered an opportunity I can't possibly
refuse.
April's stepfather needs a personal assistant.

Hunter Cash is a difficult boss.

Demanding, arrogant, challenging, but also devastatingly
handsome.
And—he's my father's rival.

I've broken all the rules already.
So, what if I break another and sleep with the enemy?
What's the worst that can happen...

ALSO BY KAT T. MASEN

The Dark Love Series

Featuring Lex & Charlie

Chasing Love: A Billionaire Love Triangle

Chasing Us: A Second Chance Love Triangle

Chasing Her: A Stalker Romance

Chasing Him: A Forbidden Second Chance Romance

Chasing Fate: An Enemies-to-Lovers Romance

Chasing Heartbreak: A Friends-to-Lovers Romance

Lex: A Companion Novella

Charlotte: A Companion Novella

The Forbidden Love Series

(The Dark Love Series Second Generation)

Featuring Amelia Edwards

The Trouble With Love: An Age Gap Romance

The Trouble With Us: A Second Chance Love Triangle

The Trouble With Him: A Secret Pregnancy Romance

The Trouble With Her: A Friends-to-Lovers Romance

The Trouble With Fate: An Enemies-to-Lovers Romance

The Secret Love Series

(The Dark Love Series Second Generation)

Featuring Alexandra Edwards

Craving Love: An Age Gap Romance

Craving Us: A Second Chance Romance

Craving Her: A Friends-to-Lovers Romance

Also by Kat T. Masen

The Pucking Arrangement: A Stepbrother Romance

The Office Rival: An Enemies-to-Lovers Romance

The Marriage Rival: An Office Romance

Bad Boy Player: A Brother's Best Friend Romance

Roomie Wars Box Set (Books 1 to 3): Friends-to-Lovers Series

ABOUT THE AUTHOR

Kat T. Masen is a USA Today Bestselling Author from Sydney, Australia. Her passion is writing angsty love triangles involving forbidden men like besties older brother.

She is also the founder of the Books Ever After store, Books By The Bridge Author Events, and spends way too much time on Tik Tok creating videos for her #1 Amazon bestseller Chasing Love.

Oh ... and she's a total boy mom.
1 husband, 4 boys, and a needy pug.

Purchase signed paperbacks & bookish merchandise.
Visit: **www.kattmasen.com**

Made in United States
Troutdale, OR
10/27/2023

14064996R00152